To Claire
with love —
Kenneth
Christmas 1962

To Claire
with love —
Kenneth
Christmas 1962

THE WONDERS OF SPAIN

THE WONDERS OF SPAIN

INTRODUCTION BY
JACQUES LAFAYE
164 PHOTOGRAVURE PLATES, 1 MAP
TEXT AND NOTES BY YVES BOTTINEAU

A STUDIO BOOK
THE VIKING PRESS
NEW YORK

Contents

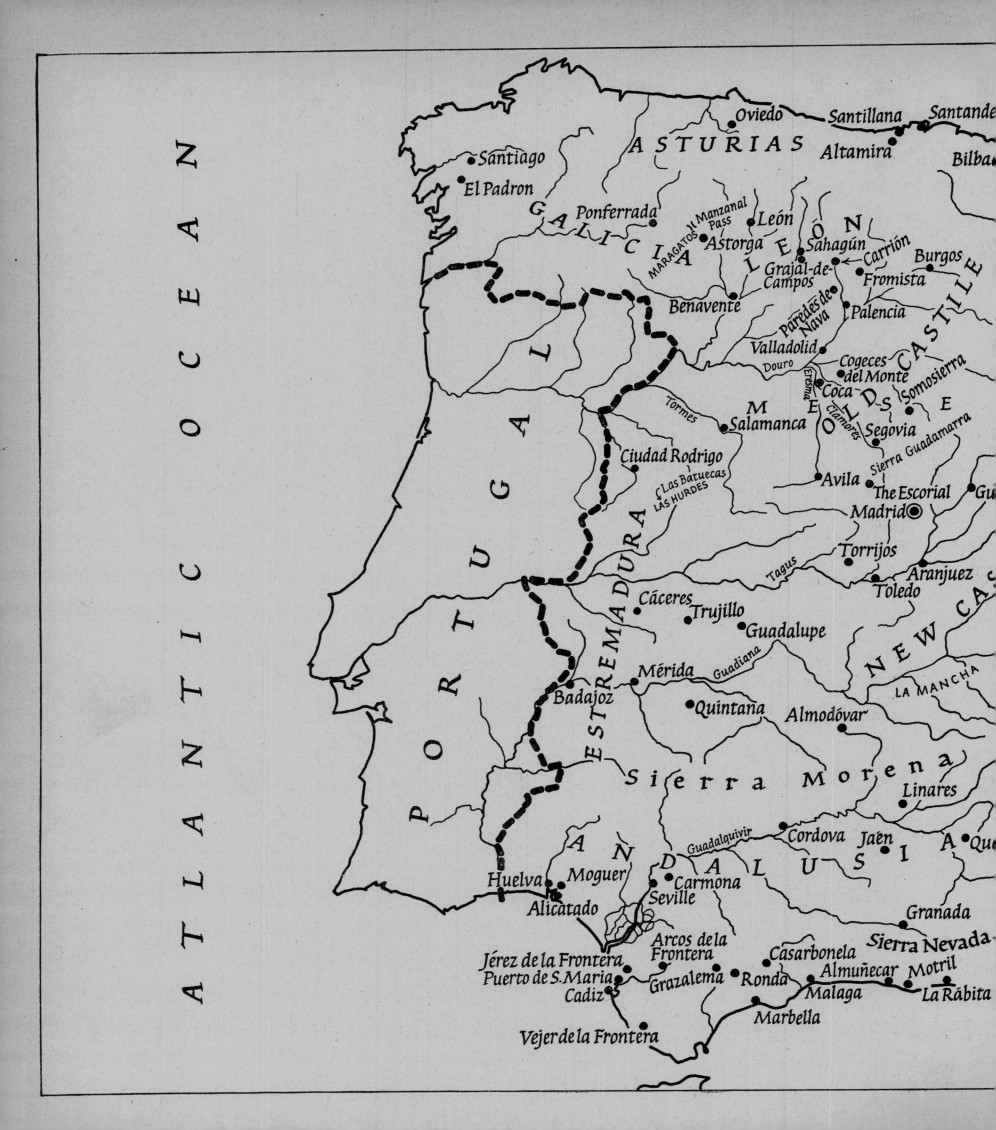

A T L A N T I C   O C E A N

Oviedo • Santillana • Santander
A S T U R I A S
Altamira • Bilba
Santiago •
El Padron •

G A L I C I A
Ponferrada • Manzanal Pass • León
MARAGATOS • Astorga • Sahagún • Carrión • Burgos
Grajal-de-Campos • Fromista
Benavente • Paredes de Nava • Palencia
Valladolid • Cogeces del Monte
Douro • Coca • Somosierra
Eresma • Clamores • O L D   C A S T I L E
Tormes • M • Segovia
Salamanca • Sierra Guadamarra
Ciudad Rodrigo • Avila
Las Batuecas • The Escorial • Gu
LAS HURDES • Madrid ◉

P O R T U G A L
Torrijos •
Tagus • Aranjuez •
Toledo •
Cáceres • Trujillo •
Guadalupe •
N E W   C A S
E S T R E M A D U R A
Mérida • Guadiana • LA MANCHA
Badajoz •
Quintaña • Almodóvar •

S i e r r a   M o r e n a
Linares •

A N D A L U S I A
Guadalquivir • Cordova • Jaén • A • Que
Huelva • Moguer • Carmona
Alicatado • Seville
Granada •
Arcos de la Frontera • Sierra Nevada
Jérez de la Frontera • Casarbonela
Puerto de S. Maria • Grazalema • Ronda • Almuñecar • Motril
Cadiz • Malaga • La Rábita
Marbella
Vejer de la Frontera

Tout est dit; on arrive trop tard.

LA BRUYÈRE

All has been said: we come too late.

ON THE SUBJECT OF SPAIN, all has long since been said. All the accepted formulae have been repeated time and time again. From the Spain of El Cid depicted by Victor Hugo to the orientalist Spain conceived by Chateaubriand and boldly portrayed by Théophile Gautier (always more painter than poet), haunted by the ghosts of the heroes of Washington Irving, tinged with an aestheticism *à la* Maurice Barrès, Spain has imperceptibly been transformed into the Spain of the Dirección General de Turismo and of the Melía Agency: a sumptuous historical setting for a boisterous festival, a never-ending carnival for the delight of succeeding generations of tourists. Condemned to the sterile contemplation of its imperial past, the Spanish people has been relegated to the outer marches of a Europe which, dedicated to prosperity, lives in a constant, though daily decreasing state of self-congratulation. Has it not been said that 'Spain is Africa', just as lightly as it has been maintained that 'Russia is Asia'? To certain ingenious minds Spain represents 'Eurafrica', a neologism which might be held to be appropriate did it not signify the rejection of a nation to which Europe is most heavily indebted for its place in the New World. Latin America is a reality, and it was Spain who made it so. The origin of the disparagement from which Spain suffers is not so much, as is commonly supposed in Spain itself, the famous *legenda negra*, or 'black legend', as the secret and alien nature of the land itself. 'Alien Spain!'—such is the title of a poem by Gabriel Celaya:

Blind Spain, my Spain,
arid, beautiful, provocative,
vast Spain, that I travel unavailingly, never to encompass you;
Spain, your pulse throbs within me,
you assert yourself the more, the more I resist you,
and you are myself without being mine, unconsciously, carnally.

A land alien to its own sons must needs be alien to foreigners. We are in the habit of substituting for a true knowledge of Spain a series of clichés—a vulgarization of famous literary creations, which may perhaps be called the 'rose-coloured' as opposed to the 'black' Spanish legend. The civil war which steeped Spain in blood in the years following 1936 led to the creation of a new version of this black legend, its roots plunging deep into the past from Las Casas to Francisco de Goya. The Spain of today—*Janus bifrons*— alternates between the Spain of the Basque drummer, the giddy swirl of gipsy skirts, accompanied by ceaseless *olés* and the click of castanets, and the tragic Spain of Hemingway and Malraux, in which the rattle of machine-gun fire has not yet died down.

The true face of Spain is to be found somewhere between these two legends, but alas, nearer to the black than to the rosy version. 'Heaven preserve me from seeing what is obvious,' wrote Blas de Otero in 1955, while Unamuno in his agony cried out, '*Me duele España*' (Spain makes me suffer), observing with bitter lucidity that '*A España la queremos porque no nos gusta*' (We love Spain because we do not like her). This reflection on the part of the man Lorca called '*El Español, el primer Español*' is the threshold beyond which understanding of Spain becomes impossible.

While the improvement of communications has demolished the Pyrenean barrier, it has at the same time raised between the tourist and the Spanish people an iridescent and impenetrable screen: the bull-fight with its paraphernalia of *fandangos*, *cuadrillos* and other out-dated rituals, the *feria* of Seville, with its tall, hooded figures and cavaliers in full regalia, flamenco songs and *zapateado* (not to be confused in translation with the tap-dancing native to another, newer world)—all these infatuate the tourist, all the more completely for the fact that the Spanish legend has prepared him for their charm. Swept into this intoxicating round, he finds his resistance further weakened by the impression that for the first time (unless he has been in Rio at Carnival time) he is seeing the streets taken over by the music-hall. Seville has become one vast spectacle. If he has eight days at his disposal, there is plenty to occupy them all. A fortnight? Then he can go on down to the coast, to Marbella, or, if he finds the heat there too overpowering, 'somewhere on the Atlantic', near the white walls of Cadiz. And next year, why not Sitges or San Sebastian? And if Sitges, then why not take in the equally pretentious Cannes or Capri? At San Sebastian in the summer season he will find not Spain but, at best, the smart set of Madrid. Tourist Spain is polarized as follows: in the east, the

Costa Brava or 'wild coast' of Catalonia and the Balearic Islands; in the west, the Cantabrian coast from San Sebastian to Santander; in the south, Seville—the more scrupulous tourists venturing over the Sierra Nevada to see for themselves Granada and the Alhambra, the snobbish undertaking the same journey merely for the sake of saying they have seen them. Similarly, Madrid, and in particular the Prado, is a tourist 'must'. Besides the abundance of Rubens and the finest Goyas, the curious may discover a handful of canvases by Bosco (the Spanish name for Hieronymous Bosch) that make the journey well worth while by themselves.

The Meseta

HERE WE LEAVE the Spain of the fairground, of the seaside and of history: three Spains of which we shall say no more, since they are quite sufficiently well known already. Here we 'must'—and this time it is a true imperative—take to the road, though Spanish roads are notoriously rare, and often somewhat improvised. Let us none the less set off along the tracks which compel us to relax our pace, perhaps necessitating a stop in some remote Meseta village, or even, far from any dwelling, on some vast and stony *pedregal*.

This is Buñuel's 'land without bread'. Without bread, not only on account of an abominable war, but by its very nature: there is no bread because there is no water. Like some enormous continental rump, barded with cordilleras rendering access difficult and crossed only by two valleys, both of them dead ends—that of the Ebro in the north, running towards the Mediterranean, and that of the Guadalquivir in the south, facing the Atlantic—the Meseta covers the greater part of the country. Though the population is sparser on these highlands than anywhere else in Europe, the very existence of Spain is due to the Meseta, enjoining unity on the richly populated and prosperous marches of Catalonia and Valencia and the Basque provinces to the north. Men from León and from Castile reconquered Andalusia from the Moors; men from Estremadura conquered and colonized America. It is always towards the Meseta that Spain has turned in her gravest hours of political or moral crisis, drawing sustenance from its very poverty. At the time of the loss of Cuba, in 1898, the Basque Unamuno, the Andalusian Machado, and the Levantine Azorín all embarked upon a discovery of the Meseta, a pilgrimage to the very source of Spain itself.

The Meseta cannot be described, it can only be experienced. The very word 'landscape', evoking as it does harmonious scenes by Patenier, Poussin or Corot, is ill-suited to Castile. It is by no mere chance that Spain should never have produced a single landscape painter—not excepting Sorolla—but only portraitists or symbolists, from Pacheco to Juan Gris, whose pseudonym constitutes in itself a profession of his faith. The line of the Sierras is the harsh back-cloth against which Velásquez has set for ever, arms in hand, King, Infante and Conde-Duque. An imposing setting for the Grandees of Imperial Spain!

The Sierras themselves, their great brows barring the horizon, represent a certain stylization, a certain kind of choice. Here is romantic Spain, haunted by the dreams of Don Quixote, a spark of life smouldering in the general *grisaille*, between boundless sky and colourless earth. From time to time cotton-like clouds appear, white promises of bounteous rain, long deferred, only to explode one day in a downpour so torrential that the sky is said to 'unleash' itself upon the earth. Antonio Machado writes of the harshness of the land:

> *Wasteland where the wolf prowls (. . .),*
> *poor and lonely country,*
> *with neither paths nor inns.*
> *O poor country accursed,*
> *poor countryside of my native land.*

Spain is born of the aggressive spirit of the mountain-dwellers of the Cantabrian cordillera and of the Meseta. Machado has traced with a sure hand the portrait of the Castilian peasant:

> *Small, agile, hardy, with shrewd eyes,*
> *deep-set, mistrustful, darting, and shaped*
> *like the curve of a crossbow, in a thin face*
> *with high cheek-bones, bushy eyebrows.*

A hard-working people, extracting from the earth the chick-peas essential to the maintenance of a bare minimum of life, metaphysical in the sense that Rosinante too was 'metaphysical'—by virtue of extreme emaciation. The Castilian

> *Stems from rough nomad stock, shepherds*
> *who lead their parched merino flocks*
> *to green Estremadura, migrating hordes*
> *whose dusty fleece the wayside sun engilds.*

The dim horizon is sometimes obscured by clouds of dust, raised by the sheep mistaken by Don Quixote for armies on the march. On the never-ending flatness of the plateau, surrounded only by the silence of the stars, it is possible to stand and feel one's own existence. Footsteps die away, swallowed up into infinity. With profound insight, Unamuno recognized in Castile a monotheistic and ascetic land. Nowhere, save perhaps on the great plains of eastern Europe, can man feel his existence with such immediate intensity. '*No hay otro yo el mondo*' (There is no other I on earth), said Don Quixote.

This solitude—and solitude is a major theme of Spanish poetry—is at the root of a fundamental, spontaneous Spanish personalism for which a dozen different explanations have been proffered. The Spaniard of the Meseta feels himself to be an absolute, eternally face to face with a second absolute: the immensity of earth and sky.

The calm meditations of Luis de León and some of the finest poems of St John of the

Cross must inevitably remain alien to those who have not experienced the Castilian night, impenetrably black, spangled with stars suspended like so many shining blades, destined never to cut the thread of time. It is as though Eternity had set its mark on the Meseta. Unlike other European countries, and other parts of Spain itself, where man has engraved on nature the stamp of his own work, the Meseta—like the Andes or Tibet—has imprinted upon man its own grey and earthy likeness.

Seen from a distance, the houses of sun-baked clay or stone, fashioned out of the earth itself, are indistinguishable from natural rocky outcrops. Here and there on the rounded hills of Aragon, León or Old Castile rise the ruins of ancient strongholds, vestiges of an era of perpetual Moorish raids. Hence the epithet '*de la Frontera*' appended to the names of so many '*pueblos*'. The names of these Meseta villages, steeped in ancestral poverty, are as poetic as they are untranslatable: Villalba del Alcor, Cogeces del Monte, Otero de Herreros, Narros de Matalayegua, Villarino de los Aires. These are the villages evoked by Eugenio de Nora:

Pueblos! Smoke rises from the populous folds of the earth,
suggesting the final act of a tragedy:
dusty ruins, after so many days,
so many years of lethal civil war, so many empty centuries.

Here men are rooted in their backwardness: yet
theirs is a man's sorrow!
Broken-seeming, suffering or lost,
and the women are in labour;
there is neither laughter nor song
in the waterless land.

A cloudburst once a year is God's curse upon this land of Cain, where only ilex, robur and holm-oak maintain a precarious existence: a land for ravens and eagles. Men huddle closely round the rare spots where water is available. Of the cities of old Spain— Avila, Sigüenza, Cáceres—where the swords of conquest were forged and the wool of the merinos woven, there remain only castle ruins, sleepy squares and great cathedrals— perpetual offerings to tempt the tourist.

Antonio Machado has evoked the desolation of Castile:

Hard, ungrateful land, my beloved land!
O Castile, your crumbling towns!
The bitter melancholy
of your sombre solitude!

Staunch Castile, harsh earth,
Castile scornful of fate,
Castile of suffering and war.
Immortal land, Castile of the dead!

This niggardly and accursed land (the Spanish *tierra* signifies both land and motherland) is all the dearer to the hearts of its own people for its meanness and its malediction. When the peasant of the Meseta speaks of his homeland, it is not Spain he means, but Old Castile, La Manca, or Aragon, a land he accepts, with resignation, exactly as it is:

> *Where there is wine, you drink wine,*
> *where there is no wine, fresh water.*

The Meseta is a land where money changes hands for water. Transported on mule-back in *alcarrazas* or big-bellied bottles, it is marketed by the glass, or rather by the draught. '*Agua . . . a! Agua . . . a fresca!*' is the cry. '*Pan y agua de Salamanca*', says a proverb.

A hardy race of men inhabits the Meseta, men always ready to throw themselves fiercely into work or combat, passionately attached to their individual scraps of land. In this land of poverty, riches are represented by the possession of a donkey, untold wealth by a yoke of oxen with which to extract from the arid soil the ear of corn which the sun will surely burn before it ripens.

By day the same sun which fertilizes the alluvial plains of the Levante and bursts like a grenade against the regularly white-washed walls of Andalusian farms, blazes implacably on the Meseta, transforming the roads into a fine dust stirred into great clouds by the feet of passing mules. In the evening it disappears over the flat orange rim of the horizon, illuminating the grey stones with rosy tints. This marks the moment for the rising of the *cierzo*, or northerly breeze—a moment quickly past, for at once the chill of night closes down on the Meseta like a lid. 'Six months of winter and six months of hell,' is the saying in Madrid. The contrast between successive seasons is as extreme as the alternation of translucent day and rigorous night.

The people of the Meseta have been moulded by the harshness of their lives and the passing of the centuries—a people timeless because bound by immutable tradition, a unique *castizo* (meaning race rather than caste) which has never given up the struggle, but managed to survive in spite of everything: dignified, susceptible and unswervingly devoted to the freedom of the individual. '*Nadie vale más que nadie*'—no man is worth more than a man—is an unmistakable expression of the Spanish sense of democracy. No egalitarian levelling down, but true equality between men for whom the state of manhood is noble. Dignified in his poverty, the Castilian is equally ready to share his chickpeas with the *forastero* (the term applied to all Spaniards from outside the province) or with the *extranjero*, the foreign tourist passing in his car. His conversation is richly spiced with proverbs straight from Sancho Panza, revealing a realistic wisdom not devoid of a certain solemn humour. The Spaniard rarely jokes, he is more inclined to mock or tease. '*Más caga un buey que cien golondrinas!*'—the ox is always bigger than the frog. '*El pan caliente y la injuria fría*'—bread is warm but slander cold. His rejoicing is reserved for the great moments of the terrestrial cycle. '*Tripas llevan corazón que no corazón tripas*'—a full belly gives man courage, but courage never fills the belly. The main events are the threshing of the corn, the harvesting of the chick-peas and the shearing of the sheep. All efforts are united in the garnering of the scanty fruits provided by the earth to feed the village from one harvest to the next. Seasonal and religious festivities often coincide. Machado took a realistic view of the Chthonian faith of the people of the Meseta:

> *Lord—paternal today, yesterday cruel,*
> *with dual image of love and vengeance,*
> *my prayer comes to you on a throw of the dice,*
> *tossed by the wind, blasphemous and worshipping.*

The Meseta varies from the mountainous terrain of Aragon, and the sierras of Guadarrama and Morena with their high passes and spruce forests, to the wheat-covered *cerros* in the neighbourhood of Burgos and the cave-dwellings of Los Hurdes in Estremadura, which reach the very nadir of Iberian poverty, timeless and primeval.

On the banks of the rivers stretch the plains, signalled from afar by serried ranks of white poplars, fluttering in the dry wind of the Meseta. The traditional imagination of a whole people has beautified these oases, tranquil echoes of Eden in the middle of a desert, where we may come suddenly upon a scene reminiscent of a Fouquet miniature, concealed in the meanderings of some stripling river, or, as at Toledo, in the curve of the full-grown Tagus. A monastery standing in an orchard, like an unexpected corner of the Loire valley, apparently fallen from the sky!

The Meseta forms a still more brutal contrast with the golden fringe of Spain. Spain's purposefulness, the rich resources of the Spanish soul, lie neither in the palm-groves of Elche nor in the Jeréz vineyards, but haunt the high places of the plateau from Huesca to Astorga, from Burgos to Mérida, from Badajos to Albacete. The very names reflect something of the harshness of the terrain: Soria, Teruel, Calatayud, Carrión, Astorga, Quintanar, Almodóvar, Trujillo. The *Romancero* has invested these high places with a heroic halo earned by epic deeds. Don Quixote has swaggered along these paths. In fertile folds such as the plain of Granada, which forms part of the Sierra Nevada— the Sierra of the south, the noble counterpart of the northern Pyrenees—mountain Spain, once rich in captains, still produces wheat and olives. What traveller has not drunk dry wine and eaten green olives among solemn-spoken peasants in some village tavern? Their eyes alight with love, these peasants are eager to discuss the richness of their land: '*muy rica*'—meaning to them everything which is fine and beautiful. Spain is also the great sweep of olive trees, grey against the red of earth, among which sparkle like diamonds in the midday sun the whitewashed farms that dot the land from Linares to Seville. And what of the orange groves of Valencia and the white gleam of sail boats on the Albufera, the eucalyptus woods of Santander, the rice fields of the Levant, the almond orchards of the Balearics, the banana plantations of the Canary Islands? But this Spain is too well known to warrant further lingering: Debussy's gardens of Murcia and the Andalusia of the cinema—more legendary even than their legend. It is the reverse side of the legend we are here seeking to evoke.

Cities of Spain

WHILE THE DONKEY and chick-pea civilization does not stretch into the heart of Madrid itself, in Toledo it still predominates. The cities of the Meseta, which until three centuries ago enjoyed a prosperity due to commerce, weaving and the manufacture of arms—enfranchised islands in a society still remaining feudal—have slowly sunk back into somnolence, reverting, so to speak, to villagery.

This is as true of Andalusian—and mountainous—Ronda, as of Cáceres or of Sigüenza. Azorín writes of the somnolence of these vacant-seeming towns:

'For the Madrilenian, the city-dweller, nothing can compare with the refreshing beneficent silence of old, dead towns . . .' he writes. But the satisfaction he expresses is a purely aesthetic pleasure, and it is hard to recognize here the author of *Tragic Andalusia*, fully alive to rural poverty, of which the lethargy of these towns is a direct reflection.

These cities provide indeed a curious spectacle: ill-paved streets in which each house bears the dilapidated arms of some noble Spanish family. Pizarro came from Trujillo, while from cities now moribund the Olivares and the Medinaceli set forth to conquer continents. Their hereditary homes are now mere ruins, or at best museums, their descendants part of that cosmopolitan society which drifts from spa to capital, anonymous despite illustrious names.

The cities of Spain are capitals, though unlike capitals of other countries: they are the capitals of all the different Spains. Approaching Santander in a tiny train puffing breathlessly along its narrow-gauge, single-track railway, turn to your fellow-travellers carrying their poultry and their baskets of fresh fish (in Andalusia these would be leather flasks of wine) and inquire about the town just coming into view: '*Santander?*' '*Sí,*' they will reply, '*la capital!*'

The 'invertebrate' Spain of Ortega y Gasset boasts a score or so of capitals. No country in Europe is at once so varied and so to speak, monadic. In Guipúzcoa, blast furnaces squat in the green countryside. Montana is an amphitheatre centred on Santander. Avila: a cathedral square. Valladolid: the memory of a kingdom. Granada: 'a paradise refused to many'—so said Lorca of 'his' Granada, the Granada in which he was to meet his death—Granada beside the 'sighing' waters of the Genil. Or again Cadiz, ethereal and dazzling, its face set towards the Americas:

At dawn Cadiz rises naked and resplendent
from the violet sea—a long, slender white arm
which Spain, in anticipation of our coming,
stretches dreamily, from her sleep.
JUAN RAMÓN JIMÉNEZ

The cities of Spain differ as widely among themselves as do its Provinces. Only two among them—three perhaps—resemble other European cities: Madrid, Barcelona and Bilbao. Their names expressly indicate that they are cities. Barcelona is '*la Urbe*' and Madrid '*la Corte*', formerly '*la Villa y Corte*'. Madrid is a city planned on modern lines, bristling with sky-scrapers. Whether we approach by the long northern road, descending swiftly from the Somosierra after interminable miles of stony barrenness, unrelieved by the sparse grey wind-torn shrubs, or by train—a journey as tedious as the plateau is monotonous—we are inevitably struck by the absence of the slightest justification for the existence of a great capital in the midst of such a desert. And our surprise increases at the freshness of the fountains, the greenness of the parks. Like the Generalife, the Retiro and the Moncloa gardens are tended with exquisite care. In the evening the Gran Vía itself, alight with smart shop windows and flashing electric signs, is hardly big enough to contain the continual ebb and flow of strollers, dressed every day as if for a Sunday. A sombre procession; for Spaniards, even when young, are given to wearing black. In the course of it, Madrid contemplates its own image, communicating by gesture, greetings and exchange of glances. The street is the public parlour of the capital. In the smaller street of the popular quarters and at Lavapiés—or what the war has left of it—the local residents settle on the pavement, bringing out their chairs, guitars and melons—the three mainstays of the *tertulía* or circle, despite the proverb warning that the melon, 'silver in the morning, golden at midday', is 'death at night.' Idylls are born to the sound of the *jota*. In the darkness hand-claps beat out the rhythmic tragedy of a needy people dancing out its unused energy.

Up to four or five in the morning passers-by may still be encountered, their presence at such an hour in no way remarkable. At daybreak the streets resume their activity: the first to unfold their stools and set up their stands are the *churro* vendors. Do not be deluded into thinking that *churros* are mere fritters! They are a sort of coil, cut into pieces about the length of your finger and twice as thick, made from a batter mixture by some old crone in a back room or attic dark with oily fumes. A *churro* vendor in Huesca once asked me to pay him in French francs as he was 'saving up to go on pilgrimage to Lourdes'. There is Spain for you! A land of saints, cathedrals and *churros*. More than a national dish, the *churro* is a rite: the natural accompaniment to the infinitesimal cup of black coffee which is the sole nourishment taken at eight in the morning by the inhabitants of Madrid, enabling them—Heaven alone knows how!—to survive till lunchtime, which is generally somewhere in the neighbourhood of four in the afternoon.

The description by Juan de Zabaleta of a day in the life of a Madrilenian in the time of Philip IV is not yet completely out of date: though the Puerta del Sol has long since superseded the square before the Church of Our Lady of Victory as the place for the exchange of news. It is a modern '*mentidero*', or place of lies, which has no equivalent in either England or France but which plays a role somewhat similar to that of the Piazza del Duomo in Milan.

The famous Plaza Mayor—almost the only vestige of the Spanish Golden Age spared by the Civil War—is entirely different. At the foot of the equestrian statue of Philip II, maids in old-fashioned uniforms wait for their soldier-escorts attired in battle-dress. Shadowy booths are huddled under the arcades which flank the square on every side, while running westwards towards the Manzanares—dry for ten months of the year and an inexhaustible source of jokes—the vía de Toledo with its shops, bazaars and *tascas* has much in common with the populous and very Parisian Avenue d'Italie.

If we accept the theory that towns, like human beings, each have their own distinctive smell, then Madrid must undoubtedly be classed as Mediterranean: Madrid smells of frying fat—not the fried potato fat of Lille or of Boulogne nor yet the honeyed fat of the Casbah in Algiers, though the latter is perhaps its closest relative. To the smell of *churros* must be added that of shrimps, or *gambas*, while the fumes of strong, brown olive oil add a bitter pungency to the aroma of sea foods and the effluvia of a number of respectable city trades.

Madrid, then, smells of oil, as Algiers smells of cinnamon and Geneva of milk chocolate. In many respects Spain is the antithesis of Switzerland, though absence of geographical necessity is a common feature. Madrid was chosen by a sovereign, a capital imposed on Spain by a series of centralizing governments. Ever since the time of Philip II, Madrid has been the political and administrative capital of Spain. Even when the king installed his government at Valladolid (capital of Old Castile) Madrid retained the aspect of a capital and, indeed, soon resumed its former status. The 'traditionalist' régime of the *Caudillo* has embellished and developed Madrid, allowing it prerogatives which bespeak a centralizing policy. The capital now contains all the ministries, the administrative bodies and the head offices of all the great industrial concerns—whether Basque or Catalan; industry is even spreading out on the outskirts of the city. The Prado, already full to overflowing with masterpieces, has been yet further enriched with spoils transferred from various museums in the Provinces.

The traveller who arrives by air, after flying over the arid hills of Aragon and the stony steppes of Old Castile, sees below him the great cross formed by the landing strips of the Barajas airport on the outskirts of a capital thronged with sky-scrapers. He cannot but be struck by such an architectural paradox. In Madrid, even more than in Chicago, the sky-scraper is a luxury, a status symbol, totally unjustified by lack of building space in the midst of so limitless an expanse.

For almost four centuries, Madrid has reflected the imperial face of Spain; modernism, now concentrated in the capital, has no roots in a land which has remained profoundly rural and archaic. Spanish tradition demands admiration both for Madrid, with all its ostentation and modernity, and for a certain ancestral—'infra-historical' Unamuno would have called it—manner of threshing corn or ploughing a furrow. We have deliberately hastened to affirm that Madrid resembles other great European cities: for such, indeed, is its avowed intention. But beneath the shining brass plates of the great companies, behind the marble façades of its banks, lies still the Spain of yesterday (and of today)—the hermetic society of the Spanish 'iron gates'. The Madrilenian will receive you in his office, in a café, or, even more probably in his club, but rarely, if ever, in his home. In Spain, men's clubs—the only ones in existence—play as important a role as in Anglo-Saxon countries. In these clubs the Madrilenian spends his leisure hours and arranges all his business appointments. In these clubs fortunes are accumulated and régimes overthrown. In these clubs *los negocios*—every imaginable sort and kind of business—is conducted.

Whereas the English club is a tranquil haven, the Spanish club is, on the contrary, marked by the dominant characteristic of all Iberian life: it is visible to every passing eye. Half of it at least consists of rows of chairs lined up along the pavement, occupied by opulent gentlemen who contemplate the passing crowds, smoking complacently, their feet nonchalantly outstretched to receive the ministrations of the busy shoe-shine boys. Open bay-windows also enable passers-by to see other groups seated inside the club itself.

The club faithfully reflects the strict divisions of Spanish society. In Barcelona, on the Paseo de Gracia, there are clubs for manufacturers, while Madrid caters for the politicians. The Opus Dei owns properties in many towns, half-club, half-monastery—but a monastery with showers, bars and billiard tables. Seville's principal club, that of the *Labradores* (literally 'labourers', that is to say, the chief landowners of the Provinces) still determines the economic if no longer the political life of Andalusia. The real life of Spain is still dominated by the Monastery and by the Club—two bastions which have survived unshaken two diametrically opposed political régimes, Republican and Falangist.

The reverse—or rather the essential complement—of the open bays of these Spanish clubs are the closed 'iron gates' of Spanish homes. The wives of club members entertain exclusively among themselves. There is nothing surprising in this, except the extreme exiguity of the concept of 'belonging'—either to a social group or to the nobility. No religious criterion is here involved, for a Spaniard who is not Catholic is no Spaniard. The immense majority of the Spanish bourgeoisie is spontaneously Catholic. The sporadic anarchism of a few scions of noble families (depicted by the novelist Juan Goytisolo) is still far from forcing the iron gates behind which the more or less hereditary masters of Spain still tacitly decide its destiny.

Spain, today, is both picturesque and tragic. It is a nation in which the city—and Madrid is the city *par excellence*—sucks the blood of an already anaemic countryside. Political régimes are not entirely to be blamed for a society in which riches seem so great only because they stand in contrast to such utter poverty. Sixty per cent of the land, admittedly unevenly distributed, is unproductive or provides only the most meagre pasturage.

If the Spain of tradition is ever to give way to a more modern Spain, the change must come from the industrial regions, the Basque Provinces and Catalonia. One of the main aspects of the abominable civil war which ravaged Spain more than twenty years ago now, was the gulf which separates the traditionally agrarian Spain of the Meseta and the industrial Spain of the Northern Provinces.

Despite concerted efforts to develop Madrid, Barcelona remains the only truly European city in Spain. Between the Montjuich and the Tibidabo, the capital of Catalonia—its industrial quarters overflowing northwards towards Sabadell and its residential suburbs creeping up the slopes of the Tibidabo—more than amply occupies a site admirably suited to a capital. The sky-scrapers of the Plaza d'España are justified by lack of space, the animation of the streets is due not so much to the number of people as to their legitimate activity: in Barcelona leisure is no more than a momentary pause. While the port has suffered slow asphyxiation since the discovery of the Americas, the chemical and textile industries have made of Barcelona a great modern city, worthy to stand beside Antwerp or Milan. Further vaunting of the old quarters and of the *ramblas* is superfluous and can do no more than echo the description given by Cervantes in the far-off days when Don Quixote was received with pomp and ceremony in the capital of Catalonia.

The great majority of Spanish towns are not so much *villas* as *ciudades*, once strong in the enjoyment of their franchise: Calatayud, Segovia, Toledo, Cáceres. The once-white cities are now blackened by the dirt of centuries: behind their façades, mosaic-tiled patios are filled with the scent of flowers and the trickle of fresh water. Many of them seem now no more than big market towns, in whose streets and through whose gates come and go innumerable donkeys laden with great bales of hay.

Toledo offers the unusual spectacle of an eastern city in the heart of Europe: steep, narrow streets overhung by glazed verandas or by wrought-iron balustrades enclosing narrow passages exuding the same freshness as the patios—a silence broken only by the sound of water, or a fairground bustle. As is usual in hot, dry countries, crowded white-washed houses overhang the terraced streets, paved with cobbles taken from the muddy red bed of the Tagus. Children straight from the pages of a picaresque novel or from some Murillo canvas squat at play in the dust under the blaze of a pitiless and indifferent sun, or besiege the passing tourist with their eternal cry of '*Una pesetita, señor, para mi colección.*'

In Spanish cities mendicity is both a normal pursuit of childhood and the exercise of a spiritual function: far more than the mere social scourge it seems when judged by purely objective criteria. The time is not long past—indeed it survives today—when the *mendigos* (also called *pordioseros* because they beg for charity in the name of God) would recite a prayer for their benefactor in exchange for his proffered mite. The beggar will help the rich man to pass through the Gospel needle's eye. In Spain mendicity provides a counterbalance (metaphysical rather than financial) to the inequality of wealth. Formerly a guide to the blind, the *lazarillo* has now transformed himself into a cicerone for the foreign tourist—a new kind of blind man who has eyes and sees not. Yet in

Spain one has only to open one's eyes to become amazed, aghast or enthusiastic. In Spain, indifference is impossible. And if our account of it betrays a passion some may find distasteful, it is a direct result of Spain herself—Unamuno's *'agonica'*—suffering her own passion, consumed by her own internal struggles. We can only hope that the true face of Spain will emerge from among the various contradictory interpretations placed upon it, our own among them.

The Sea

WHILE THE WRECK of the Invincible Armada in 1588 precipitated the decline of the Spanish navy, supplanted first by that of England, and later by the Dutch, Spain's maritime vocation did not vanish overnight. For more than a hundred and fifty years after the Armada, the sea was to remain the principal bond linking together one of the greatest colonial empires of modern history. Not even the emancipation of Spain's American possessions in the nineteenth century—an upheaval resulting in the birth of the present eighteen states of Spanish America—dealt the death-blow to a navy which once boasted sailors such as Pinzón, shipmate of Columbus, Jorge Juan, discoverer of California, and the *Conquistadores*, bold seafarers one and all. Hernán Cortés, conqueror of Mexico, shares with the Portuguese the honour of inventing the amphibian navy. To ensure the capture of the city of Mexico-Tenochtitlán, on an island in a lagoon, Cortés ordered his men to dismantle their galleons and transport them on their own backs across the high passes of the Sierra Madre. Re-assembled and launched upon the lake of Texcoco, these enabled him to compel the Aztec capital to surrender.

The hardest blow—to national pride rather than to Spanish naval power, then already long upon the wane—was the defeat suffered by Admiral Cervera in 1898, honourably vanquished by the modern fleet of the United States. After the loss of Cuba and of the Philippines, the vast Atlantic empire of Philip II was reduced to no more than the Canary Islands, first stepping-stone on the path to the New World.

Technical progress (cold-storage ships, trans-oceanic airliners) have today made these islands a favourite site for the cultivation of bananas and a natural 'stop-over' for inter-continental airlines. Tropical islands, within easy reach of Europe, inhabited by the hospitable Guanches—so mysterious in origin that they are even held to be survivors of the lost Atlantis—their lunar landscape still liable to volcanic eruption, the Canaries are doubtless destined to enjoy a magnificent future as a tourist centre: a promise already showing the first signs of fulfilment.

But the once mythical, now merely picturesque charm of these islands should not make us forget the history of the old world. The Mediterranean empire carved out by the twin kingdoms of Aragon and Catalonia in the Middle Ages suffered by the discovery of the Americas. This discovery led to a westward shift of the great commercial axes of the world, formerly passing through the famous ports of call of the Levant. The Isabelline Palaces in Valetta on the island of Malta still bear witness to the sojourn of Spanish builders.

While the vital role in America was always played by Basques, the collapse of Spain's Mediterranean empire served to convert Catalonia to industrial activity. The rise first of Genoa and then of Marseilles, the absence of a sufficiently rich and spacious hinterland, led to the slow asphyxiation of the port of Barcelona. Manpower, however, is still to hand, and should the paths of commerce one day pass again through Spain, a race of mariners, sons of the sailors of Lepanto and Navarino, are ready once more to prove their seamanship. It was their forefathers, in pursuit of Barbarossa, who first constructed, on the island where now stands the Admiralty, the Peñon of Algiers— a dagger pointed at the heart of the Berber city. The maritime vocation of Spain cannot be better symbolized than by Cervantes wounded at Lepanto, and Lope de Vega sailing in the Invincible Armada. In the Mediterranean, Spain has kept the Balearic Islands, their splendid southern rusticity not yet wholly ruined by tourism. In the Balearics and the Canaries Spanish naval tradition is still preserved intact. Meanwhile, the renewed prosperity of the Basque shipyards testifies to a renaissance. Here freight-carrying has restored to life the Spanish merchant fleet, while the naval shipyards of Cadiz in turn are beginnning to enjoy a revival of activity. The future of the Spanish flag upon the high seas seems assured.

Meanwhile, suspended between memories of eternal glory and the still modest hope of future strength, Spanish seafaring is devoted first and foremost to the fishing industry. If the shepherd of Avila—anonymous representative of the agrarian masses scattered over the high desolation of the Meseta—represents one of the truest images of Spain, the Spanish fisherman must surely be recognized as the second mainstay of the country. The Cantabrian fishermen, the tunny-fishers of Cadiz, even the eel-catchers of the Albufera, still constitute the main reserve of manpower for the Spanish merchant fleet. The sardines of the Basque coast, the crab and salmon of Cadiz or Huelva, the red mullet of the Balearics constitute, together with the ubiquitous *mariscos*, the staple food of the coastal populations.

In a country divided by the great sierras, served by an inadequate railway system, the possibility of eating fresh fish at all times and in all places comes as a pleasant surprise. Together with the *tortilla* (a kind of well-cooked, dry potato omelette) the *merluza* is a recurrent item on the bill of fare of every Spanish restaurant. We are obliged to admit, however, that even after many years of peninsular life we are still unable positively to identify the *merluza*. According to the class of restaurant, the term may be used to describe the most succulent of pollock or the dreariest of whiting. Spain possesses as many varieties of *merluza* as of olive oil. For those of our readers not given to gastronomy, further commentary will be superfluous. Suffice it to say that—particularly where the results are liable to be the most dire—fish, eggs and cereals constitute the great trinity of Spanish sustenance, always inseparable, of course, from the olive oil of Andalusia. The sea, however, also provides culinary delights: for instance *paella*. A gastronomer-friend from Granada—the region boasts many such discerning palates—assures us that *paella* must be eaten on the sea front of Valencia, where the salt sea breezes add an indispensable touch to its savour. The Castilian *puchero* (a kind of stockpot stew) pales besides this riot of seafood, tiny fishes, rice, pimentoes, meat and poultry, the choice and exact proportions of its ingredients being left to the discretion of some esteemed matron of the Albufera.

The fishermen of Spain, braving heavy seas to bring back hake and mullet, rare treasures in these waters, deserve our especial admiration. They have but limited resources; their boats are obliged to sail till they can sail no more. Their precarious existence is threatened as much by universal poverty as by wind and storm; witness the line of women waiting on the quays, the joy at the first glint of shining scales.

In Cantabrian villages, houses huddle in narrow streets decked with washing or with bunting—like a Dufy painting of some Provençal 14th July—their glass verandas overlooking the fleet of trawlers gathering in the evening light. Tall houses, under a low and cloudy sky, towering in a semicircle round the waters of a creek, or in twin rows along the river bank: Ondárroa, Bermeo, or, perched high above the Costa Brava, San Pablo de Mar, or Cadaqués—meeting place of Salvador Dali and García Lorca. Fishing villages such as Zarauz or Tossa, living in a cycle of seasonal prosperity, or tourist centres such as Santillana, are still dependent for the most part upon the tunny catch, the seething glitter of the sardine shoal, a harvest secure only when the silent stream slithers upon the quay.

The South

WHATEVER OUR APPROACH TO SPAIN, sooner or later we must come to Andalusia. Since we refuse to condone the paradox of a Spain shorn of its celebrity, we shall forthwith—to use a most un-Spanish idiom—take the bull by the horns, and speak of Andalusia.

Let us then amble no faster than a mule along the red and dust-strewn paths, flanked by hedges of aloe and of prickly pear—our lungs filled with the cloying sweetness of the air. The scent of orange blossom, which has retained the arab name of *azahar*, mingles with that of rosemary and all the fragrant flowers of the ancient garden of the Caliphs: carnations blooming by the wayside, carnations tucked among the tresses of the Andalusian ladies.

Such is the Andalusia of Federico García Lorca, whose *cante jondo* was born of inside knowledge of Andalusian exuberance.

Italy and Spain are often lumped together in a single Mediterranean category. Yet

Naples and Seville are poles apart. The gestures of the Andalusian mime the tragic destiny of a land surfeited with sun, a land of olives and of bitter wine—sherry and manzanilla. Andalusia is an avalanche of olive trees and vines between the rocky slopes of the sierras. The villages are not so very different from those of the Meseta, though more southern and with white-washed walls: Grazelema, Isnájar, Vejer de la Frontera. The sun, synonym of joy in the mind of nordic races, here flashes its merciless rays on scenes of proud poverty or violence. Listen to the *Cante jondo* of Federico García Lorca:

Pueblo,
On the bare hillside
a Calvary.
Clear water
and age-old olives.
In the alleyways
hunched men,
and on the bell-towers
weathercocks turning,
turning
eternally.
O lost pueblo
in sorrowing Andalusia.

This tragic reflection of a reputedly 'laughing' country is in no way peculiar to the genius of the poet. While Goethe, Heine and Gautier have all sung the praises of '*das Land, wo die Zitronen blühn*', their joy is no more than the aesthetic pleasure of the traveller far from his misty homeland. For, in Andalusia, the sun's rays are like so many dagger thrusts. To feel the secret tragedy of a city like Seville, perpetually represented in holiday guise, we must cross the Triana bridge at night. Like a thousand others, this bridge is a metal structure spanning the Guadalquivir between Seville and Triana, marking the site of an ancient act of murder: 'Other knives are useless. Other knives are blunt and fear blood. These we sell are cold. They plunge deep, seeking the warmest spot, and there they stick.' It is no mere chance that words so symbolic of bitterness should have been written in Andalusia, penned by the hand of the most *gitano* of all the poets. Is it so very far from such prose to the flouncing skirts of the *gitanos* of the Sacro Monte? These are the twin faces—sensual and macabre—of the 'tragic Andalusia' sung in his youth by the poet Azorín.

What does the flamenco *cantaor* sing, if not the absolute and mysteriously ubiquitous distress of a people in perpetual exile? A survival of medieval monody and plainsong, the *jondo* has also inherited the modulation of Koranic prayer: an echo rising from the darkest depths of time or from the very bowels of the earth, like this song of the miner of Almadén:

'Oh . . . o . . . o'
A miner lamented,
Deep in a mine.
'I am in such solitude!
Only a lamp with me.
I am alone . . .'

Even in its more joyous manifestations such as the fandango or the Sevillana, flamenco is stamped with a sacred gravity.

The mobile face, the changes in facial expression, the rhythmic clapping of the spectators, the vocal encouragements addressed to the dancer, all stimulate her to the achievement of unconscious perfection. Hence the term *ambientado*—for Spanish, like German, has a word to express self-forgetful collective joy, in which the spectator becomes a part of the general spectacle. The general participation which makes primitive dances so irresistible survives in jazz and in flamenco. Dancer and singer dominate the spectators from the crest of the wave of enthusiasm which they have inspired in them.

Rhythm is the only discipline of a melodic inspiration which carries the human voice to its utmost limits.

But the clash of castanets and the sensuality continually promised—but never actually granted—by the dancer does not drown the hum of the guitar.

Down the years the sound of the guitar of Pepe Escalera seems to come faintly to our ears, mingled with the shrilling of the cicada, in the gold and purple sunset light of Moguer, where waving vineyards and umbrella-pines surround the little farm of the poet Juan Ramón Jiménez and his donkey Platero:

'The sunset is crimson-tinged, wounded and reddened by its own flashing light. Its splendour revives the pinewoods, flushing them with pink; and the flowers and grasses, translucently kindled, imbue the serene instant with their moist scent, light and pervasive. I remain enraptured in the twilight.'

To Juan Ramon's *finca* came young poets to 'try out' their inspiration. It is said that one Spaniard in every two is a poet. But any irony is here misplaced. Every *cabal* or true Spaniard is—as Chénier would have said, at least—'a poet at heart'. As far as we know, Spain and lands of Spanish civilization are the only places in the western world where poetry is 'tried out' in much the same way as plays are tried out elsewhere. Ever since the Italian Renaissance, in societies dominated by a commercial bourgeoisie, poetry has been an expression of feelings of revolt or failure.

Whether doctor, *abogado* (a term including not only barristers but every kind of lawyer), dancer, shepherd, intellectual or winegrower, every Andalusian carries within himself a spark of inspiration, his own particular *ángel*, and a high awareness of his human dignity.

Peevish spirits may still maintain that Spain is no more than a paradise for beggars. We, for our part, have undertaken to show Spain in so far as possible as she really is, and not as she appears to foreign tourists at the gates of Spanish palaces and within their very precincts: the home of licensed mendicity. The Spanish people are dignified in their poverty, proud to the point of violence, choked by a creative spirit perpetually deprived of outlet. In the words of the unknown poet of *El Cid de Bivar*:

How good a vassal, had he a good lord!

So much for the people of Andalusia . . . But the South immediately evokes the names of southern cities: Granada, Cordova, Malaga, Cadiz, Ronda and, of course Seville, of the Andalusian dream-world. With his usual insight and concision, Lorca has hit upon the truth: 'Seville recounts the happenings at Granada'. Seville, with its María Luísa gardens, is an artificial paradise, a theatrical setting for boisterous festivals.

It is rather at Cordova, in the heavy silence of a summer afternoon, that one may catch the rhythmic beat of the secret heart of Andalusia. True, its narrow streets, irregularly paved with cobbles, cannot always match the careful stylishness of the Barrio de Santa Cruz in Seville. But with its blinding white façades, its patios musical with fountains of fresh water, the aristocratic hauteur of its barred windows, Seville is Seville. The real Andalusia is to be found in Cordova, true capital and greatest of all the Andalusian towns. Seville, like Valencia or Barcelona, is a city, whereas Cordova, though densely populated, has remained merely a good-sized market town. Cordova should be seen on fair days. With bursts of Andalusian fire, dealers dispute the price of a mule or of a litter of young pigs. Boleros, flat-crowned hats and the highly picturesque if tattered local version of the universal cap mingle in an atmosphere heavily charged with animal excrement.

Cordova is the southern sister of Burgos, Salamanca and Avila. Built beside a Roman bridge linking it to the surrounding countryside, it is still haunted by some mysterious oriental presence. Toledo is a caravanserai. Cordova, on the other hand, evokes the Orient of the harem and the mosque at prayer time. From its heyday as the capital of the old Caliphate, Cordova has retained, in the quarter immediately adjacent to the mosque, a slightly stiff grace, in contrast to the rustic character of the poorer quarters.

At Cordova, mountain-girt,
at Seville, sea-tanged
and rustic, with a sail
billowing towards the ocean;
and in the wide plain
where the sand
soaks up the bitter froth of the sea . . .

Thus Antonio Machado links the two southern capitals. Seville is, of course, a port: in the sixteenth century it enjoyed a monopoly of trade with the West Indies, and occupied a position comparable to that later held by Amsterdam or Antwerp. Out of the immense wealth of its past, Seville has retained its towers, its cathedral, its gardens and its noble houses: the Barrio de Santa Cruz. Whereas in Barcelona—as in Paris, Innsbrück or Casablanca—superb villas stand in their own parks on the outskirts of the city, the sacred precincts of Seville lie within the walls—or what remains of them— of the Alcázar itself. Here the Dukes of Alba rub elbows with foreign diplomats, absentee landlords and successful politicians.

The Barrio de Santa Cruz has nothing of the chilly stuffiness of the bourgeois quarters of most of our great cities, nothing of the expensive whimsy of our residential suburbs: it remains an aristocratic legacy from the Spanish Renaissance, in which the influence of Palladio is often happily combined with nine centuries of Judeo-Moorish tradition.

Night takes on the intimacy of a small square,

wrote Lorca. Within the Barrio de Santa Cruz are concealed many small squares, where the scent of jasmin and of orange blossom floats in an exotic halo round the bracketed lanterns, illuminating glimpses of flowered patios, rich in pools and jars of flowers . . . It is the Seville of the *Arabian Nights*, whose praises have been sung so often and in so many keys by artists ranging from Théophile Gautier to Luis Mariano.

No comment can do justice to the overwhelming charm with which the great Andalusian city strikes the visitor, who, unlike the tourist, stays long enough to live with the Sevillians, to absorb the quintessence of the Barrio de Santa Cruz, purged of what must in all honesty be called its affectation. The second tourist attraction of Seville is the Calle de las Sierpes, the street where all the world and his wife go walking in search of summer shade and winter sun. It is a mixture of the Paris boulevards, the Gran Vía of Madrid and something else, indefinably but unmistakably Sevillian. The spirit of Seville is not to be found in any given spot: time alone reveals the secret of a city which chooses always to wear the mask of levity.

Let us therefore now pay homage to the gods of modern travel and turn our attention to the Seville *feria*. This brings us to quite another chapter of Spanish history: the complex and legendary history of games sacred and profane. Indeed we must ask ourselves the question whether, despite the profanations of modern publicity, such games are even now ever entirely profane in character.

Games Sacred and Profane

ALTHOUGH IN SEVILLE Spanish festivals sometimes degenerate into a fairground spectacle, they are as a rule essentially spontaneous. Isolated from the rest of Europe by the hostility of its neighbours or by a voluntary withdrawal, and internally divided by its natural relief, Spain has maintained intact certain strong provincial traditions of which its games and festivals are the most attractive feature.

Every Spanish town has its annual *feria*, much in the same way as every French town boasts a special culinary delight, and every German town a local industry. Holy Week in Seville, the Feast of San Isidro on 15th May in Madrid, San Firmin on 7th July in Pamplona, the March festival of the Fallas in Valencia, that of Our Lady of the Pillar at Saragossa, the less famous Holy Week festivities in Valladolid, and everywhere, of course, the Carnival. The occasion is always a Saint's day, generally that of the patron saint of the locality, whether of city or of village.

It is, in fact, in the villages that it is easiest to grasp the spontaneous nature of the *feria*, which can, however, on occasion assume truly remarkable urban splendour. But wherever the *feria* takes place, its meaning and its manifestations are almost always identical. Despite its religious origin, it indulges in the profane delights of merry-making, calling upon every facet of the wide range of Spanish talent.

The Virgin, Saint or effigy of Christ is carried in procession with great ceremony, greeted by cries of 'Hail to the Virgin of Sorrows! Hail to our patron Saint! All hail!' to the accompaniment of thunderous applause. The sacred image is escorted by *guardia civil* in their statutory leather cocked hats, preceded by dignitaries of Church, State and Army—village priest or cardinal, mayor or provincial governor, captain of local constabulary or officer of the general staff. Children line the way, inquisitive or merely bewildered, while adults—men and women alike—follow the procession, bearing candles and chanting hymns of praise.

One original feature of these processions, especially vigorous in Seville, is the ceremony of the *saeta* or 'arrow of song': an impromptu lyric directed at the sacred image by one of the spectators. At once the procession draws to a halt and, amid general silence, preceded by a roll of drums similar to that which in the circus ring heralds the most daring exploits of the acrobats, the voice of one of the faithful rises in invocation and prayer. The melody is improvised in accordance with a certain poetic rhythm, but the theme is always that of fervent religious devotion.

At Seville, in particular, these processions are embellished with truly anachronistic splendour. Long files of penitents draped in black hoods—the Nazarites, worshippers of *Jésu del Gran Poder*. Lorca's description is full of baroque vigour in the finest tradition of Spain:

> *Into the narrow street*
> *come strange unicorns.*
> *From what country,*
> *from what groves of mythology?*
> *Nearer, and they are like astronomers.*
> *Fantastic Merlin*
> *and* Ecce Homo
> *Durandal bewitched,*
> *crazed Roland.*

Here we are on the borderline between the sacred and profane, but where Lorca merely hints, Blasco Ibáñez, the novelist, shows no such restraint: 'Every fifty feet or so the sacred image draws to a halt. In many houses people ask that the Virgin should stop so that they may have a longer look. Every café keeper has insisted on a halt at the door of his establishment, invoking his rights as a local resident. Of course there must be a stop. Here is the finest *cantaor* in the world, who wishes to aim a *saeta* at the Virgin! 'The finest *cantaor* in the world, supported by a friendly arm, hands his glass to a neighbour and advances unsteadily towards the statue; clears his throat and unleashes a stream of raucous notes. The drums roll on behind the image, and the trumpets launch their high lament, and everyone sings at once, merging their discordant voices, each man beginning and ending his *saeta* when he will, without consideration for his neighbour, as if everyone had been struck deaf, or as if each man felt himself isolated by religious passion, shorn of all external signs of life save for his voice vibrant with adoration and his eyes fixed with hypnotic intensity upon the *paso*.

'When finally the songs die down, the public bursts into obscene demonstrations of enthusiasm, continuing to glorify the *Macarena*—the beautiful, the unique *Macarena*, who makes all other Virgins jealous: and glasses are filled with wine and handed round at the very foot of her image, and the most enthusiastic toss their hats to her as if she were a pretty girl, and no one any longer knows or cares whether the true festival consists in the fervour of the songs of praise to the Virgin or in the pagan orgy accompanying her procession through the streets.'

The dominant trait of Spanish devotion is its esoteric character. The most remarkable example is doubtless the Apostle St James, riding his white horse to render assistance to the Spaniards in the battle for the reconquest, or in the far-distant Peruvian adventure of Renaissance days. But the people of Saragossa still worship the Virgin of the Pillar, those of a certain quarter of Seville adore the *Macarena*, those of another, *Jésu del Gran Poder*. Idolatry of sacred images is carried so far that faithful Sevillian worshippers of the *Macarena* shut their windows in the face of the *paso* from a neighbouring parish in sign of protest.

Nevertheless, in so delicate a matter it remains unwise to draw sweeping conclusions from such isolated instances. The cult of images is, however, carried to great lengths throughout the peninsula: witness the Christ of Burgos made of human skin, crowned with thorns and splashed with human blood. The cathedral of Barcelona offers to the worship of the faithful the image of the Christ of Lepanto who turned aside in the hour of battle to avoid a cannon ball.

In the Provincial Museum of Valladolid, which houses the incomparable *Magdelene* of Gregorio Hernández and several works by Berruguete—the El Greco of Spanish sculpture—a Spanish lawyer-friend pulled out his handkerchief and wiped the coagulated blood seeping from a polychrome effigy of Christ, remarking, without any undue emphasis, that 'you would think it was real flesh'.

The Spanish Christ is a man who suffered crucifixion. The God of northern peoples, less exteriorized (God the Father, perhaps, rather than God the Son), more frequently praised in song than in image, probably offered more propitious material for the spread of the Reformation; a feature to which sufficient prominence has not been given in the attempt to explain the scant success of Calvinism in Spain. It is all too easy to take refuge behind the screen of fire and smoke raised by the *autos-da-fé* of the Inquisition.

The Spaniard places himself on the same plane as God himself and all the Saints of heaven, often teetering on the edge of blasphemy by dint of excessive familiarity and susceptibility. A personal bond binds the believer to his Saviour, who is also a man, and a man who suffered. He worships him and implores his intercession, even, on occasion, bitterly reproaching him for his indifference if the favour is not granted.

Lope de Vega—religious poet, priest, Knight of Malta and Member of the Holy Office of the Inquisition—led an extremely unconventional existence, continuing to write light comedies and even to supervise their production. Though times have changed, the tendency remains the same. The churches of Spain are still the scene of public displays and passionately fervent demonstrations. St John of the Cross danced before the altar and St Teresa of Avila composed love poems to 'the All-Divine'. Why, therefore, should the cobblers of Triana hesitate to toss their hats to the Virgin as to a successful matador? We should refrain from treating as superstition or as blasphemy what are, in fact, fundamental expressions of Spanish religious fervour, for such gestures have received endorsement from the most saintly.

Since Christ is above all a suffering human, offered up in sacrifice, why should we be surprised to see his cult associated with the ancient Cretan rite of tauromachy, the Manichean struggle of Man and Minotaur? In every town and village of Spain the *feria* is the occasion for a *corrida de toros*, often with public participation—that is the unleashing of the bulls in the public thoroughfares, as at Pamplona for the festival of San Firmin. Those who condemn such games—if indeed they can be called a game, for certainly they are no sport—with the reprobation rightly reserved for any act of collective barbarism, must in all honesty consider their implications. The passes of the matador's cape demonstrate the self-discipline of a man who, by retaining his composure, can completely dominate a brute beast, rendered furious by deliberate provocation, even, on occasion, by blazing and exploding *banderillas*. As in Picasso's *Guernica*, the beast is symbolic of the unseeing and unbridled force of evil. The good people seated round the bull-ring itself, or in the stands under the blazing sky, for many hours before the *corrida* begins, have come to see the bull not killed but vanquished: hence the merciless volley of cat-calls and broken bottles aimed at the unhappy matador who butchers his bull. When this happens, it is the bull who is the hero, and the *torero* who is called murderer, butcher or, sarcastically, a melon!

To vanquish the bull requires the observance of a ritual which is far more difficult, and more dangerous. Many great matadors—Manolete among them—have met their death in the arena. Lorca has celebrated the glorious death of one of them in his *Lament for Ignacio Sánchez Mejías*:

> And the song of his blood flows on
> over the marshes and the grasslands,
> trickling from the embedded horns,
> searching, uncertain and soulless in the mist,
> enveloping a thousand muzzles,
> like a long, dark, sorrowing tongue,
> flowing on to form a pool of starlit death
> by the banks of the Guadalquivir.
>
> . . .
>
> *No, I do not wish to see it.*

The composer Maurice Ohana has set Lorca's text to music with great originality, but in a profoundly Andalusian spirit. The perfect harmony of the two works expresses most powerfully the tragedy of a 'game' in which man risks his life in single combat, a second Christ for the redemption of mankind, a fighter in continual jeopardy. For if he fails to kill according to the rule, it is the *torero* who is vanquished, and with him the spectators, who revile him as a traitor. The example of the famous Belmonte and his master 'El Gallo', who retired to their country property after long years of triumph in the ring, constitutes an all-too-rare exception.

In spite of disgruntled affirmations to the contrary, our own era possesses some fine 'swordsmen': Luis-Miguel Dominguín, Ordóñez and others. Those who refuse to acknowledge this are often supporters of the school of Manolete, the sobriety of whose style has remained exceptional. Bull-fighting is, in fact, divided into two major trends, one classical in its sobriety, the other more expressionistic. There are, however, three different schools: those of Seville, Ronda and Madrid. But this whole concept remains vague, and a *torero* who has risen to the heights of glory often imposes his own particular style and creates his own disciples. However this may be, no one would think of killing the bull just in any manner: he must kill it as a man: deliberately, coldly, after leading it step by step to the exact spot and moment chosen in advance for its defeat.

For want of knowledge of a technique which is exceedingly complex, and also because such a study would be out of place in the present context, we shall not enter here into the subtle details of the art of tauromachy. In his sacred function, the matador commends himself to the good graces of the Virgin before the combat; his friends pray for his life and the chapel is as integral a part of the arena as the bull-pen.

One of the surest signs of the rapid 'Europization' of Spain is the progressive though still relative abandonment of the bull-ring, at least in the great cities, in favour of the football match. It is indicative of Spain's remarkable power of absorption that even in the dictionaries the word is spelled '*fútbol*'!

The *toros*, however, remain if not the national sport at least the great Spanish 'game'. In the breeding farms of Andalusia (*ganaderías*) crowds gather to watch the *tientas* and the *novilladas* in which the young bulls bred for combat are tested simultaneously with the budding champions of the *plazas*. Here owners, managers, matadors and *aficionados* meet to prepare for the coming season.

But nothing is so picturesque as the village festivals, where the main square—its exits barred by temporary palisades—is transformed for the space of a few days into an improvised arena for the local matadors. On the day itself, the patron saint is carried in procession, merchants sell mounds of the multi-coloured almond paste called *turons*, as well as *tortas*, *cocas*, *rosquillas*, *churros* and pancakes. In the taverns and on the doorsteps of the houses, those inspired by local wine—in Spain always dry and often faintly redolent of gun-flint—dance a *fandanguillo* or sing a *jota*. There is never any lack of amateurs to strike up on the guitar—the gipsy *solear* or *siguiriya*, if we are in Andalusia. While the Spanish people, personalist (but not individualist) to a very high degree, finds its noblest incarnation in the person of the matador, braving death alone in the presence of thousands of spectators, the festival of San Firmin at Pamplona reveals a complementary aspect of the Spanish genius. Once a year, starting on 7th July, Pamplona lives in fear throughout the week! A contrast is often drawn between the north of Spain, more moderate, and southern Andalusian fire. But while the *feria* of Seville consists of a parade on horseback or in carriages, a display of traditional costumes, San Firmin is an orgy of every kind of sport, the main attraction of the whole *feria*—night and day alike—being the unleashing of the bulls in the open city streets. To diminish the danger, their horns have been previously bandaged. Excited by the crowd and the applause, the young men of the district—peasants from the neighbouring mountains, workmen from the town itself, or students on vacation—brave the bulls at as close quarters as they dare and then endeavour to escape their horns. More than one pays dearly for his temerity with a heavy fall, and sometimes with more serious injury. Dances start up in the corner of every square and gangs parade the streets.

Such communal rejoicings are the rule in Spain. The Spanish people are continually gathered in the churches to hear Mass, in the fields to thresh corn, or on building sites for work, and spontaneously assemble on every kind of sacred or profane occasion.

If the *corrida* is essentially sacred, then so is Carnival—however profane it may outwardly appear. In Pamplona, again, and in many other peninsular towns, Carnival is celebrated with incomparable splendour. What has become a Bacchanalia in Munich or in Rio, a society romp in Nice, has preserved its traditional character in Spain. As in the Middle Ages, it is the signal for carousal and for miming the disorder of a topsy-turvy world. The grimacing faces of the giant figures carried through the streets are covered in the Moorish *djellaba* worn by the ancient enemy. The curious mixture of masks, parochial banners, priests with croziers, white-robed choir boys, *guardia civil*, and parading bands heralded by a heavy roll of drums, pierced by the shrill notes of the trumpets, combine to give the Spanish Carnival a unique aspect.

To single out one province in particular would be to do injustice to the other ten. Valencia, the great metropolis of the Levant, celebrates St Joseph with an unequalled profusion of chandeliers, flowers, costumes and huge baroque images or *Fallas*. Madrid launches its bull-fighting season on the feast day of its patron San Isidro.

Corpus Christi in Granada, on the other hand, is marked by calm solemnity, contrasting strangely with the noisy disturbances of Seville and other Spanish cities. 'Granada has an aura of mystery: something impossible yet true,' declared Lorca, returning from New York in 1931.

We have already spoken of the sadness, evoked the sunlit tragedy of the south, and recalled the high significance of the kill. All this is an integral part of Spain, part of a people whose distractions are wilder than those of any of their neighbours, a people moved, but on rare occasions, by an irresistible collective outburst of feeling. The rest of the year the Spanish people take their pleasures sadly: singing with accents gramophone records alone can capture, escaping as they do the notation of the stave.

Let us listen for a moment to the oriental and Ronsardian notes captured in the lyrics: between each sung verse, silence or the murmur of the lute:

> *In the orchard,*
> *I shall die.*
> *In the rose-garden*
> *They will kill me.*
> *I went, mother,*
> *To gather roses;*
> *I found my loves*
> *In the orchard.*
> *In the rose-garden,*
> *They will kill me.*

This lyrical, almost-accomplished folk-song is anonymous, as are many Spanish masterpieces. Here too we may discern the mark of Spain's Catholicism. The Church of Spain (both temporal and spiritual) is a subject which we can no more avoid than the matador can escape the ultimate encounter with the bull. And the link is here far more than metaphorical: the Cross and the bull are the twin symbols of Iberian passion.

The Church

WHETHER HE LIKES IT OR NOT, the foreign visitor to Spain is certain to be struck by the number of priests he encounters on the roads and railways of Spain, their rôle in public ceremonies, and the respect with which they are regarded. While some will ascribe this to the excellence of a clergy still able to lead the masses into the path of prayer, and some praise the beneficial effects of a strong spiritual tradition, others again will admit only the illusory triumph of political and social pressure. These interpretations are far from exhausting an extremely complex subject. Any effort to understand the Spanish Church involves an attempt to penetrate to the heart of the history of the Spanish people.

First under the Romans and subsequently under the Visigoths, the Church provided the Iberian peninsula with doctrinal unity. At the time of the first Council of Toledo, in the year 400, the Church imposed itself as the main spiritual force in Spain; and until very recent times it has been responsible for all important political and administrative appointments. It was the monks who colonized the territories reconquered from the Moors, even fighting side by side with the soldiery. Priests confessed both kings and people. The Dominicans rooted out heresy and the mendicant orders followed hot-foot upon the *Conquistadores* to the Americas, conquering expressly to banish superstition by the conversion of the Indians. The eighteen republics of Spanish America still bear living witness to this spiritual conquest.

In the far-off days of the early Middle Ages, when the Kingdom of St Peter was in process of disintegration, the Bishop of St James of Compostela claimed to be the legal custodian of the eternal truth. At the time of the Lutheran and Calvinist schisms, Spain took up arms for the preservation of undivided Roman Truth in Europe. The Society of Jesus, successor to the Order of St Dominic, was created by a Spaniard, Ignatius of Loyola, for the restoration of the Roman faith. Cardinal Cisnaros, one of the promoters of Spanish unity early in the sixteenth century, acted as Regent until the accession of Charles V. Philip II was famous for his piety. Nor should we be deluded by the apparent diminution of the political influence of the Church in Bourbon times. For, except during the 'enlightened' reign of Charles III, the Church has always played a decisive rôle in the destiny of the Spanish people.

In a less political sphere, it should not be forgotten that Spain possessed one of the most popular places of pilgrimage in medieval Europe—the shrine of St James of Compostela. Spain is also the country of St Isidro of Seville, of St John of the Cross, of St Teresa of Avila and the Blessed Luis de León, to mention only the most famous. Spain can produce Catholic letters patent of nobility in comparison with which even those of France and Italy must seem to pale a little. The jurist Vitoria, the theologians Vivès and Suarès were all monks.

It was in Spain that the first polyglot Bible made its appearance: the Bible of Alcala, a university rivalling even those of Salamanca and Paris. Profane literature can boast the Archpriest of Hita (a combination of Rabelais and Mathurin Régnier), Tirso de Molina, a Brother of Mercy, and the great Lope de Vega, who came to the priesthood late in life. Some of the greatest names of the theatre stand beside those of the most famous chroniclers of the West Indies: the Jesuit Acosta, Brother Bernadin de Sahagún;

Father Las Casas who defended the Indians against the *Conquistadores*-turned-tyrant; Brother Antonio de Solís y Ribadeneyra—he has also been identified with Brother Juan d'Ortega—who became the leader of the Hieronymites and author of the famous picaresque novel *Lazarillo de Tormès*.

The Church of Spain—or more strictly speaking the Spanish clergy—represents the entire spiritual, political and intellectual activity of Spain, including the most profane as well as the most sacred literature, from the fifth to the eighteenth century. Though the rôle of the clergy seems to have become a more self-effacing one in modern times, we are in no way surprised to find that the Church nevertheless remains at the root of the numerous decisions affecting the whole future of the country. It required the rise of socialism, communism and, above all, anarchism for Spain to become the scene of any anti-religious manifestations. The bloody division of Spain into 'Reds' and 'Whites' is one which fails to take into account innumerable instances of deep personal conflict. The majority of the Spanish people will consent to shoulder arms only when they can claim that God is on their side.

The Church represents primarily the force of tradition, but it also inspired new traditions through the agency of Francesco Giner de los Ríos, the lay reformer and founder of the *Institution Libre de Ensenanza*, and master of Antonio Machado. Don Miguel de Unamuno must probably be accounted somewhat heterodox, but his Christian inspiration can no more be called in doubt than that of any 'integrist' Catholic; and certain of Lorca's poems, vaguely classified as 'surrealist' until recent studies revealed their mystic inspiration, are in the true spirit of traditional Catholicism.

It is impossible not to be dazzled by the profusion of cathedrals, chapels, cloisters and priories built by Spain in the course of her many centuries of Catholic faith. A few names outshine all others: Burgos, Toledo, León, Salamanca, Avila, Segovia, Valladolid on the Meseta; and elsewhere Barcelona, Palma de Mallorca, Seville, Cadiz, Cordova, Granada and, in the extreme north-western corner, St James of Compostela—a very forest of romanesque arches and gothic casements. Nor must we omit the two cathedrals of Saragossa: the Metropolitan Church of the Pillar and the '*Seo*'. Whether pure romanesque like St James, or French gothic like León, all Spanish cathedrals are remarkably monumental. The majority, like Seville or Salamanca, built by slow degrees or rebuilt after a variety of disasters, show a combination of styles: gothic, plateresque and, finally, though more rarely, Jesuit. Cordova presents an unparalleled monstrosity: the transformation of mosque into cathedral, at a period when the opposition of Spain and Islam was no longer a matter of life and death for Spain. Rather than wax indignant over such a breach of taste, allegedly due to 'innate' Spanish fanaticism, let us attempt to estimate (though no assessment given here can be other than very incomplete) the over-all artistic contribution of the Spanish Church. We have already spoken of the main cathedrals. Mention must also be made of the monastery at Yuste where Charles V retired, the cloister of Sigüenza, the Charterhouse of Miraflores, the monasteries of

Poblet in Catalonia, of San Cugat, of la Rábida in Andalusia, whence Columbus set out on his journey to America, of San Lorenzo in the Escorial, in which Philip II meditated on the fate of man, and of San Juan de la Peña, whom legend associates with the Holy Grail. In the style of Spanish churches the influence of Citeaux and Palladio, of Moorish and of French gothic converge in a soaring monumentalism, expressive of the sublime aspiration of the Church of Spain towards an all-powerful Deity. The spirit of the Gentle Shepherd invoked by Blessed Luis de León is more apparent once inside the cloister walls.

These two tendencies, apparently contradictory but in reality complementary, are also to be found in the carving of Spanish capitals and tympanums. And what of the Barcelona museum with its countless polished or polychrome effigies of Christ carved in wood and stone? The monks of Zurbarán, the religious paintings of Ribera and Herrera—many of which hang in the Prado or in the *Real Academia des Belles Artes* in Madrid—the El Grecos in Spain as well as those in the United States, all testify to the fact that the plastic arts, like architecture and literature, owe a considerable debt to the Spanish Church. For was not the Church—to put it bluntly—the principal, if not the sole patron of Spanish painters, architects and sculptors?

Such is the fantastic and overwhelming heritage of the Spanish clergy of today. Foreigners are inclined to accuse the Spanish Church of worldly compromise and interference in political life. Such phenomena merely perpetuate a state of affairs which has long been in existence. Was it not the Church which drew up the plans for the cities to be built in the New World, according to the norms of Aristotle's *Politics*? Is it not the Church which in practice still dispenses knowledge to the children of Spain? Whenever it proves inadequate to the task, it is from within its own ranks that the most vehement protests are raised. Towards the middle of the eighteenth century, in a series of essays collected under the title *Teatro crítico*, Father Feijóo, a Benedictine of Oviedo, took up the cudgels against false miracles, and denounced a decadent scholastic teaching which had become incompatible with the modern scientific spirit then in the ascendant in France and England. The fight against superstition has always been led by churchmen. And superstition—in its peculiarly Spanish form of Quixotism—is more prevalent in Spain than in most other countries.

'For a true Spaniard, there is no such thing as an improbable miracle,' wrote Gabriel Celaya. The real miracle of the Spanish Church lies in its tenacious hold upon the country. The Church is as deeply embedded in Spain as a finger-nail in the surrounding flesh. In Spain sacred office is held in far greater respect than in any other country, yet the Spanish clergy as a whole has remained in closer contact with secular life. The church is still a public meeting place, a theatre for profane performances. In accordance with the old adage, 'Church, navy or the household of the king', Spanish noble families still send their younger sons into the service of the Church as a kind of natural tribute.

In Spain, the Church both wields the power and leads the opposition. History is full of the struggle for power among the great religious orders. The appearance of the Jesuits heralded the eclipse of the Dominicans. The Mendicant Orders monopolized the early stages of the evangelization of the American Indian, though the Jesuits later succeeded in securing a foothold and in creating the dissident theocracies of Paraguay. Suppressed and subsequently re-established, the Society of Jesus, approved by the Pope in 1540, played a major rôle in the history of modern Spain. It now seems possible that its brilliance may eventually pale beside the rising star of the Opus Dei.

Modern Spain is the work of the Spanish Church. Any attempt to sketch a portrait of the Church in Spain today would be a hazardous enterprise: perhaps the safer course will be to efface ourselves behind a selection of pictures of the people and the country over which it has for so many centuries held undisputed sway.

Spain Past and Present

But the eternal quality of a people remains viable
only in forgetfulness of its historical quality,
with all its exclusiveness.

MIGUEL DE UNAMUNO

'TOMORROW IS ANOTHER DAY' (*Mañana será otro día*)—the Spanish phrase for putting off until tomorrow what can be done today, or for deferring the consequences of present actions, has deep roots. One of the most remarkable minds of the great liberal generation, Professor Américo Castro of Princeton University, sees in this the influence of Islam. For the Christian, the Creation is a phenomenon that is completed, for the Moslem it is perpetually renewed. The real meaning of '*Inch Allah*' is 'Why worry about tomorrow? God will provide.' Addressed to someone else this becomes 'Come back tomorrow' (*Vuelva Ud. mañana*)—tomorrow, that is to say one day, some *other* day. But the concept 'one day' is conveyed in Spanish by the expression '*cualquier día*', and, in point of fact, means never.

Such a euphemistic dismissal often perplexes non-Spaniards who, for their part, have no time to waste. Spain, on the contrary, has been wasting time for centuries, so what difference can it make to waste another month, another hour? In Spain, time is eaten up by every gesture reproducing a thousand eternally repeated gestures: the peasant flailing the corn, the priest celebrating mass, the gipsy singing a *solear*, the fisherman's wife eternally knotting the same knot as she mends her nets, the matador aiming and re-aiming the fatal sword-thrust.

In the Europe issuing from the industrial revolution 'time is money'. Nations of robots live in the shadow of the foreman-timekeeper, their noses glued to the assembly lines of mass production. The Spanish people are a free people, enjoying a freedom far more radical than those boasted by their neighbours—whose liberty of association, liberty of expression, are no more than ostensible breaches in the solid wall of technological and administrative slavery.

In Spain, time must no doubt be considered relatively unproductive. What practical interest could there be in calculating the 'lost time' which the Germans or the Belgians would struggle to regain?

How many hours a year are spent in prayer? The Church has all Eternity before it. How many hours are killed by the thousands of idle soldiers? Foreign conquest forged the arms which, weary of awaiting an occasion for new exploits, turned finally on Spain herself. How many calories expended in singing and in dancing? A fertile earth, ships, mines and workshops are required to provide work for all the idle hands in Spain. Meanwhile Spain has time and to spare for personal reflection and for hunger: land-hunger leading to agrarian communism; work-hunger, and hunger for bread and wine, engendering anarchy and revolt; hunger, too, for action and for glory, which breeds the matador, the artist, the leader and the saint.

The epic deeds of the medieval knight El Cid or of his caricature Don Quixote, represent a momentary flash in the dark night of Spanish time. Spain is not a country of slow, continuous effort, in which the passing years multiply the efficacy of gesture and the result. Spain keeps its energy intact for impossible adventures, for violent spasms, for strokes of genius or of folly. In a world in which courage is useless without technology, Spain is condemned to ostensible sterility. Unamuno's cry, '*Que inventen ellos!*'— Let others do the inventing!—relegates Spain to that 'infra-history' in which it is still slumbering.

In a vacuum of industrial sterility the ancient heritage of Spain awaits the great revolutions or spiritual mutations of tomorrow. Of all the nations of Europe, Spain is the most likely to provide Bergson's 'indispensable complement of soul' without which the industrial world is threatened with self-annihilation. When progress begins—or resumes —its forward march in Spain, technology and production will at last truly become weapons in the service of mankind.

But the Spanish people are held captive by the chains of history. The rivers of Spain are spanned by Roman bridges, bridges across which stormed the Arab hordes— Omayyads, Almohádes and Almorávides—advancing from the south in pursuit of Vandals, Alans and Visigoths, who, coming from the north, had preceded them in Spain. The heterogeneous splendours of ten centuries of Islamic domination are followed by a Catholic Golden Age equalled only by the Renaissance in Italy. So many artistic treasures, so many architectural masterpieces: Spain is a museum for the foreign tourist, a prison for the modern Spaniard. From within the glass cage of a past persistently glorified in the name of 'tradition', Spain contemplates a distortion of its true reflection: its history is the battle raging ever since the Middle Ages between the partisans of the open door and the stubborn defenders of the sepulchre of El Cid: the true Spain is not yet born.

Rome, Islam and Judaism, Cistercian Catholicism, Franciscan Italy, German mystics and Flemish masters made of Spain a melting pot of races, techniques and doctrines from the second century BC until the seventeenth century AD. Then she became stultified in her own imperial grandeur. The nostalgia resulting from the gradual dismantling and disintegration of the Empire remains one of the principal motives of present Spanish policy. Officers on half-pay, armchair reformers, enlightened monks, the crowds which throng the bull-ring, the tens of thousands of emigrants who leave Spain every year are all waiting, each in his own manner, for the arrival or revival of a more or less chimerical Spain, above all of a Spain which will no longer cause them to suffer.

Tomorrow

'TOMORROW WILL BE A NEW DAWN,' wrote the poet Gabriel Celaya in 1955, endeavouring to introduce a note of promise amid the discouragement induced by the continual deferment of a Spanish future. Today he is no longer a voice crying in the wilderness. After a parenthesis of some fifteen years of anarchy and civil war followed by persecution, Spain is now, in spite of everything, experiencing a renewal, though a whole generation—the generation of the Civil War, the fighters, the massacred and the exiles—is missing from its present glory.

The Spain of yesterday stretches out to the Spain of tomorrow the hand of welcome:

> *You are not the dead,*
> *You are the new young,*

wrote Rafael Albertí in 1937; Albertí, who with Lorca and Sasona was the great dramatist of the 'liberal Golden Age', as it has been called by Juan Marichal.

The generation of 1930 and that immediately preceding it—Azorín's 'Second Golden Age' of Spain—saw the renewal of traditional poetry achieved by Antonio Machado, the somewhat Mallarméan modernism of Juan Ramón Jiménez (who received the Nobel Prize in his Puerto Rican exile two years before his death), the neo-Kantian philosophy of Ortega y Gasset, the universalism and encyclopaedic erudition of Miguel de Unamuno, the international fame of Dr Marañon, the revelation of the medieval past by Menéndez-Pidal; these alone ensure the glory of Spanish letters for the first half of the twentieth century.

But this first flowering was followed by a second crop of genius destined to be decimated in blood and chaos or dispersed in an often voluntary exile. Lorca, assassinated in Granada; Miguel Hernández, dying in prison of tuberculosis; Rafael Albertí and Alejandro Casona exiled in the Argentine, Manuel Machado in Chile; Luis Cernuda in Morocco; Pedro Salinas dying in America; Jorge Guillén, settled in France and subsequently in America—such was the fate of poets alone.

Manuel de Falla died in the Argentine. Paris is now the home of a second Falla, Maurice Ohana, native of Casablanca, who has maintained the continuity of a tradition dating back to the *Cantigas* of King Alfonso, his traditional but inventive style contrasting with the radical innovation of Bartok or Stravinsky.

Spanish history, philosophy and *belles lettres* are represented in Mexico by Victor Alba and Salvador de Madariaga, in the Argentine by Ramón Gómez de la Serna, in the United States by Américo Castro and in France by José Bergamín. The cinema has Luis Buñuel in Mexico, while in France the theatre is represented by the great artist María Casarès, daughter of the former Spanish president, Casarès Quiroga.

Modern Spanish painting may almost be said to have become French, but without ceasing to be profoundly Spanish: witness both the pictorial work of Pablo Picasso and his employment of a pottery technique inherited from the Catalan and Valencian masters of the Middle Ages. Cubism was created in Paris by the Spaniard Picasso with Braque, and Juan Gris (José González of Madrid) influenced its development in the 'synthetic' phase. Their mighty figures have somewhat overshadowed painters such as Grau Sala, Figueras and Clavé who certainly deserve more than passing mention. Another major trend of modern art—surrealism—is brilliantly represented by a Catalan, Joan Miró. Lastly, another Catalan, the outlandish Salvador Dali, who with his disconcerting but wholly deliberate absurdity must be considered one of the more curious products of our day.

In his compatriot Casals 'Spain in exile' possesses one of the greatest international virtuosos of our time.

Thus the influence of a decapitated Spain—or rather of its severed head grafted on to the native thought and art of France and South America in particular—since it was they who welcomed or accepted the majority of exiles—has been of great importance, though the exact limits of its action are difficult to define.

The contribution of the Spanish nation to the outside world during the last half century is somewhere in the order of several million emigrants—with or without the blessing of authority. There are more than two hundred thousand Galicians in Buenos Aires. Countless Basques are now living in South America, mainly in the Argentine. Algeria and south-western France have provided work for many Spanish immigrants. Spanish legionaries fought under the French flag at Narvik, and Spanish masons are still employed for the building of French houses. By present reckoning, some sixty thousand persons a year are leaving Spain—if indeed we can give credence to any estimate of a persistent flow yielding neither to controls nor interdictions.

> *. . . without dancing or song*
> *they are departing, leaving the dying hearth*
> *as your long rivers, Castile, flow to the sea!*

wrote Machado, who left Spain to die at Collioure in 1939.

Despite losses which benefit neighbouring countries, it is inside Spain that the Spanish future is now being moulded with implacable determination, a renaissance which refuses to be stifled. Among those remaining to carry on amid the ruins runs a clear expression of a will for survival and renewal.

The poet Gerardo Diego, Dámaso Alonso—also a poet, but above all a prince of critics—scholars like José Manuel Blecua, Samuel-Gili Gaya or Rafael Lapesa, and historians like M. Jiménez Fernández are inextricably bound up with their native land: the indivisible yet widely varying land of Cossío, painter of Santander, and the Meseta of Palencia and Ortego Muñoz—a land to which, wrote Cossío, 'it can never be said that I owe much, since, indeed, I owe it everything'. These men represent the 'deepest permanent factor of Spanish painting: realism, a realism of feeling, the realism of Velásquez and of Zurbarán—which is also the realism of the artist who wrote these words, Rafael Zabaleta, 'the Picasso who stayed behind'. Living in a remote village of the Sierra de Quesada, Zabaleta provides dazzling proof that Spanish energies are by no means exhausted by the academic productions of the less distinguished followers of Sorolla, the Spanish Manet. The intervening age, that of 'loyalist' as opposed to 'red', or Republican, Spain, was shaped, or rather mutilated, in the fire of battle. It is a Spain which numbers not a single master. The death of the Falangist theoretician, José Antonio, sacrificed by the politicians of the movement, left a serious gap. The political thought of contemporary Spain oscillates between the 'Spain without problems' of the integrist monarchists and the 'problem Spain' of Laín Entralgo.

The Spain of the future is not yet born, but its outlines are already discernible in certain trends of Spanish thought, both secular and religious. While the silent Xavier Zubiri, who is accorded the reverence due to a prophet, restores Christian philosophy to the transcendental plane to which Heidegger, one of his masters, has restored philosophy as a whole, he must nevertheless be ranked as one of the pre-war generation.

Post-war Spain, the Spain of the children who were the terrified witnesses of the battles of a fratricidal war, is now sounding for tomorrow the knell of the great division:

> *I speak not of ruins, nor of hate and anger,*
> *even though anger, hatred and destruction haunt and pierce me;*
> *In my soul I bear the cross of my smoking country,*
> *but above arises a clear star,*

proclaimed Eugenio de Nora in 1950. Echoing the poet, Victoriano Crémer places the renaissance under the sign of Ruben Darío, writing of rebellion and of life in his *New Songs of Life and Hope* (1952).

Poetry is deeply ingrained in Spain. Blas de Otero and Carlos Bousoño, young offshoots of the old *castizo* trunk, claim descent not only from Lorca but from Antonio Machado, whose poems provide the most perfect evocation of his country; an Andalusian ardour concealed beneath the half-tones of the Meseta.

While young painters such as Tapies, Millares or Saura draw inspiration from international non-figurative art, those forming what may be called the Madrid school—Juan Guillermo, Ochoa, Menchu Gal or Redondela—are among the undoubted descendants of the realist tradition whereby 'Castile confers an unmistakable stamp on all things Spanish'. (R. Zabaleta.)

The advent of a film director such as Juan Bardem, worthy to stand with the very highest, including his compatriot Luis Buñuel whose inspiration contrasts so strongly with his own (the miracle of the camellia flowering in the desert); the genius of Ataulfo Argenta, one of the 'born leaders' of our century, dying too soon; the discovery in the course of an unpublicized recital of a young virtuoso, A. Roderíguez Baciero: all these are further proof of the vitality of Spain which will one day break down all barriers.

Catalan employers, the young priests returning from visits to France or Belgium with a new conception of their mission, the formidable power of the Basque Bank, the even more formidable silence of a whole nation muted for so long, and, above all, the Spanish earth, so vast and so unevenly distributed—these represent a potential which, given political direction, is capable of revolutionizing the features of the Spanish 'problem'.

The gentle poet Juan Ramón Jiménez will never see the future he invoked in 1910:

> . . . *mother*[*land*]
> *Poor, grave, ravaged!*
>
> .   .   .
>
> *face to the sun*
> *which will rise for you tomorrow,*
> *your soul prostrate, yet young, ardent,*
> *earth bearing lions,*
> *flames in place of walls.*

As this poet has prophesied, the Spain whose future has so often been deferred will, on some not far distant day, burst forth into new atmosphere—'an ideal, pure air, at the centre of the atmosphere, as it were its soul.' (Jiménez) The 'new wave' of the men of today, preceded by what Jorge Guillén has called the 'clamour' of the men of yesterday, will sweep it forward.

But, alas, the birth of Spain is a never-ending process. How many times before, when all seemed ready for a new epiphany, has Spain relapsed into the old ways.

But, today, as Eugenio de Nora wrote in 1953,

> *The children would regain the heritage of their age.*

and Time, though still weighing heavily on Spain, is surely preparing in the shadows the harvests of tomorrow.

The Spanish Earth

Todo yace en mudez; ninguna señal llega de la campiña.
De eterno confiesan estas tierras haber sido pobres y se
disponen a prolongar otra eternidad su miseria.

*Everything lies dormant; there is no sound from the countryside.
For an eternity these lands have confessed their poverty, and they
are resigned to yet another eternity of misery.*

JOSÉ ORTEGA Y GASSET
Castilla y sus castillos

SPAIN, together with Portugal, forms a continental mass at the extreme western point
of Europe: the high plateau of the Meseta, flanked by mountain ranges, the depres-
sions of the Ebro in Aragon and of the Guadalquivir in Andalusia . . . But why enu-
merate such fundamental facts? Is it not better to evoke the land of Spain in a series of
poetic impressions, showing how men, beasts, trees and flowers combine to compose
a single song, so splendid and unique that we never tire of hearing its innumerable
verses.

So many landscapes to be discovered, not only devoid of human presence, but untouched by human hand! The immense and stony stretches of Castile are apocalyptic
in their desolation. In Estremadura the rhythmic undulation of earth and hill suggests
the respiration of a province sunk in slumber. Sometimes, as though seeking consolation
for its solitude, the earth has transformed the rock itself into a semblance of human life
or the outlines of a city. Thus fifteen miles from Cuenca, rises the 'enchanted city' with
its palaces, squares and streets, giants and monsters. It is not difficult to imagine some
magician's hand chiselling this fantastic universe through the centuries, seconded by
the ceaseless hammering of the wind.

F—WS ENGLISH

Here the links with earlier stages of human life—prehistoric, pre-industrial—have not yet been severed. The sheer perfection of the cave art of Altamira—with its astonishing renderings of animal life—still excites the admiration of the twentieth-century visitor. In the Valley of Las Batuecas, in the pitiful region of Los Hurdes, practically isolated from the rest of the world for many centuries, there still exists a physical and moral poverty more usually associated with darker, more remote periods of history. Near Astorga, in the sad and desolate country of the Maragatos, on the slopes of the Foncebadón and Manzanal passes, many villages still seem to date from Islamic times. In a never-to-be-forgotten setting near Calatayud in Aragon, on the road to la Soledad gape the mouths of cave-dwellings. Seen from the road, their inhabitants are like scraps of the pitiful red earth, simultaneously called to life and condemned to everlasting misery by some caprice of divine will. And how many similar dwellings can be instanced!

It would, however, be unfair to linger indefinitely on such scenes of misery, when other scenes equally austere and wild, but at the same time far more human, are awaiting us. All along the road of Spain—highways and country lanes alike—unfolds scenery of biblical grandeur. In Castile, in Estremadura, in Aragon, flocks of sheep endlessly roam the denuded plateau, watched from a distance by shepherd and sheepdog—a sight so frequent as to be commonplace. The shepherd's face is tanned and seamed by the wind and the sun. Occasionally a sheep-bell sounds, its silvery note striking the hostile bronze disk of the sun.

But need we, like José Ortega y Gasset, evoke only the eternal poverty of the tragic expanses of Castile? These should not lead us to forget the rich cornlands, the big villages clustered round their great churches, broad enclosed farmlands, and the sight, in summer, of the blinding clouds of red dust, straw and sunlight swept along by the strong wind of the Meseta.

Nor should we forget more idyllic landscapes, whose sweetness tempts the hearts of passing lovers to an enchanting halt. By flowing river or still lake, tall trees screen the sunlight, or at least interpose their leafy spires between its brilliance and the earth; flocks graze in the meadows; and with evening, an exquisite freshness falls upon the air. We find undiscovered villages and hidden corners worthy to provide Don Quixote's Dulcinea with the rustic setting so delightfully described by Cervantes.

Time has forged innumerable links between the land and its inhabitants. Many towns and villages have taken on the colouring of the surrounding plain or mountainside as though claiming protection of the earth's maternal mantle. Above all, the topography of Spain furnishes an admirable explanation for the character of its inhabitants. Were it not for the relief of the peninsula, which is both unified and appallingly divided, it would be impossible to understand the complex course of Spanish history, tending always towards unity, but often branching off at a tangent in response to the violent particularisms of the old kingdoms, or of the great natural geographical regions.

The seductiveness of Andalusia, the severity of Castile are inseparable from the Spanish temperament. Antonio Machado wrote:

> *My childhood is memories of a patio in Seville*
> *and a bright garden where lemons ripen;*
> *my youth of twenty years in the lands of Castile . . .*

and this poet's work shows a great attachment to the countryside.

Miguel de Unamuno has not only acknowledged but proclaimed his love of nature, saying that the love 'felt for nature both by the intelligence and by the heart is one of the subtlest products of civilization and of culture.' He maintains that work in the fields teaches a man to love nature, and that the fruits of the earth create in man's heart the feeling of gratitude. This, however, must be dominated, for its full value is achieved only 'when man has made himself master of those favours of the earth to which he was formerly a slave.' The great writer declares his preference for the 'wide, austere, solemn' landscapes of Castile, the earthy villages which seem to spring directly from the soil itself, sharing the very contours of the country.

Thus the Spanish earth, because it is harsh and wild and arid, because it grudges man even a bare subsistence, has set an indelible seal on the soul of Spain. It constitutes an essential element of what Miguel de Unamuno has called 'the profession of being Spanish'.

Notes on the Plates

1
PLATEAU
SURROUNDING
CIUDAD
RODRIGO, LEÓN

It is appropriate that this selection of pictures of Spain should open with an almost boundless landscape, suggesting in itself a meditation on infinity: the characteristic of Spanish earth is to lift its face to heaven. Here we have the symphony of cloud, earth and town. Almost the whole horizon is filled by the sky, the earth is reduced to a narrow sliver; the town rises from a fold in the ground, forming an austere parallel. In this practically unlimited expanse and from this compulsory contemplation of nature, Spain and its inhabitants have learned that God gives unstintingly of the splendour of his Creation, and that the heart of man should also learn to give and never count the cost.

León is intimately connected with Castile—topographically and, perhaps even more, by its military history. The distant glimpse of the town of Ciudad Rodrigo may suggest that to our meditation on infinity, we should add a thought for heroism. Situated not far from Portugal, the town played an essential role in the long struggle between first Castile, then Spain and their Iberian neighbour. Naturally, it possesses a magnificent cathedral, a number of noble houses and picturesque streets: its atmosphere is eloquent of peace of soul and martial valour.

2–6 THE FRUITS OF THE EARTH

2
OLIVE GROVES
OF BAÑOS DE LA
ENCINA

The activities of man here portrayed could surely serve to illustrate a second *Georgics*. Here olive trees, not clouds, fill the horizon with their quivering multitude. At a glance all the trees seem identical. Yet each has its particular way of bending and sighing in the wind, of holding its leaves to the golden sunlight: at evening they are reddened by the setting sun, at nightfall they become a myriad of shadowy shapes retreating softly into the encroaching darkness. The olive groves of Spain are a silent and immovable army, defying the merciless alternation of sun and night.

The proximity of the Atlantic may be deduced from the abundant rainfall and the near-tenderness of the light, so that Galicia appears more smiling and more fertile than it really is. This land is very different from the endless stretches of Castile, León or Andalusia. Among the mountains, on the borders of the forests lie meadows set with clumps of trees. At the sight of the peasant following his oxen-drawn plough a host of literary allusions spring to mind, enhancing the serenity common to all rustic scenes. Virgil would have loved this wide expanse of noble country, where the work of the fields has remained unchanged throughout the centuries. We may imagine a shepherd, a poet or musician, playing his pipe in the shadow of some broad tree; and dream that this gnarled and ancient trunk could have inspired La Fontaine to write his fable *The Oaktree and the Reed*. But here literature is leading us astray . . . for we are in Galicia, where the earth is harsh and life arduous for the peasant.

A visit to the Ebro delta region at the southern extremity of Catalonia is both delightful and instructive. The alluvial deposits of the river, on their seaward journey, have worked their way more and more deeply into the old city of Tortosa, with its cathedral dating from 1347 and almost modern *Lonja* or city market. The commercial capital of the delta is, however, now Amposta. Ever since the middle of the nineteenth century great efforts have been expended on the reclamation of these marshlands, with drainage, the elimination of malaria, the cutting of canals and the development of rice fields. The population has considerably expanded. Man's determination and ingenuity have thus extracted the very utmost from this watery region, into which order and productivity have been introduced without in any way destroying the originality of its character.

Here man's obstinacy has been applied to the dryness and irregularity of the Spanish earth. Low walls have been built in order to retain what little fertile earth there is, so that at least a part of the former wild expanse now bears the stamp of a geometrical pattern traced by the hand of man. Only the assiduous care of generations of peasants preserves the soil from the renewed onslaughts of a hostile nature.

The Huelva region, in eastern Andalusia, is famous for the richness of its sub-soil; in its northern region are the mines of Río Tinto. A flat and monotonous stretch of country, broken only by the last bastions of the Sierra Morena, is here given over to the cultivation of the vine. For many weeks the bunches grow daily heavier in the ripening sunshine, each grape transformed into a miniature sun, till suddenly, at harvest time, the interminable rows of vines become the centre of a swift burst of activity. From these vineyards come famous wines, particularly Manzanilla, so pleasant to sample in some delightful side-street of Seville.

7–10
**STOCK-RAISING
AND PASTURAGE
IN THE SPANISH
COUNTRYSIDE:**
near Arcos de la Frontera
(Plate 7), Scala Dei (Plate
8), in the neighbourhood
of Jaén (Plate 9) and of
Santa Magdalena (Plate 10)

The remarkable thing about these four plates illustrating stock-raising and pasturage in Spain is not their reminder of one of the principal resources of Spanish economy, nor yet the particular nature of the animals portrayed, but the impression they give of a way of life which is impressive and archaic, some twentieth-century survival from the Middle Ages. Jaén and Arcos de la Frontera are situated in quite different parts of Andalusia, while Scala Dei—famous for its Carthusian monastery—and Santa Magdalena are both in Catalonia. Yet to all intents and purposes the atmosphere is the same: the animals wander over the stony surface of the earth as though on some age-old migration. Only an occasional peasant-woman grazing her goats beside a country road reminds us, perhaps, of some more familiar corner of French countryside.

11
**CHURCH AND
PALM GROVE
AT ROCAMORA**

Palm groves may evoke in the mind of the traveller not only Spain—but also another continent, conjuring up visions of the enchantment of Africa. However the mere sight of palm trees is enchantment enough: their motionless fronds apparently resting upon the air, their towering trunks barring the sky. A blinding light bathes the whole land-scape in the joyful innocence of some lost paradise: the humblest dwelling is transmuted by the sun into a flower of dazzling whiteness.

12
**THE RIO SEGRE
NEAR LA SEO
DE URGEL**

The town of La Seo de Urgel, once a great religious centre, boasts a romanesque cathedral begun by a team of Lombards in the second quarter of the twelfth century. Surrounded by a number of remarkable churches and monasteries, it stands at an alti-tude of over two thousand feet, on the right bank of the River Segre, not far from its confluence with the Valira, flowing down from the high valleys of Andorra. In this Pyrenean region, the divisions imposed by the relief explain the independence of the mountain valleys and the erstwhile importance of townships like La Seo de Urgel. Look, for instance, at the Segre, which must here traverse some twenty miles of impressive gorges, opening out from time to time into a broader valley. Once the timber felled in the great mountain forests was floated downstream on its waters. Improved communica-tions have diminished the isolation imposed by nature, and the complications created by relief, revealing these Pyrenean valleys to the outside world. It is possible now to understand the problems formerly confronting their inhabitants and forming the very basis of their history.

Montserrat, some forty miles from Barcelona, a famous place of pilgrimage, offers also mountain scenery of rare and majestic beauty. The ridged and gullied hillsides, streaked with belts of vegetation, bear a curious resemblance to human heads resisting encroaching baldness. Roads, funiculars and cable railways enable excursions to be made to the grotto of the Virgin, the chapels of Santa Cecilia or San Miguel, and above all, to the highest peak, San Jerónimo, more than 3,600 feet above sea-level, which provides a tremendous panorama extending from the mountains to the sea.

**13
THE ROCKS OF
MONTSERRAT**

Grazalema is situated in the north-eastern part of the Province of Cadiz, on the road from Arcos de la Frontera to Rondo, in a mountainous region which lends the town enchantment. It follows the slope of the hills, the tiled roofs of the churches and the houses matching the colour of the rockface, so that it seems as if earth, men and town lived in a kind of symbiosis admirably conveyed by the broad fresco of this picture.

**14
GENERAL VIEW
OF GRAZALEMA
IN ANDALUSIA**

This is not, as it appears, the beach of a mysterious small cove, still harbouring an obdurate band of wreckers surviving from the brave days of sail, but merely an unfamiliar corner of the port of Malaga—a city of almost 300,000 inhabitants, scaling the slopes of the rocky coastline, with busy port, charming streets and languorous perfumed gardens. Not far from the freighters and the liners, the steel hawsers and the smoking funnels, it is still possible to find a few yards of virgin shore, where the swing of the waves keeps up its changeless rhythm and where boats, drawn up upon the sand, bear witness to the persistence of the humble, age-old activity of the fishermen.

**15
MALAGA**

Only a sand-bar connects the rocky isle of Peñiscola (Castillón de la Plana Province) to the mainland. It has been occupied successively by the Templars and by the Knights of Manresa, and it is fortified on every side. The castle itself, monumental and magnificent, includes a courtyard commanding a sweeping view over the Mediterranean, a church dating from the latter half of the thirteenth century, a Tower of Tribute, halls

**16
PEÑISCOLA**

and dungeons. When Christendom was divided up among the rival popes it was to this lonely promontory that Benedict XIII retired in 1415. His obedience was reduced to nothing more than the castle and island, yet he died within the castle walls, a few years later, secure in the conviction that he was the one true Pope.

**17
ROAD FROM
MOTRIL TO
MALAGA:** view of the
Cerra gordo

The road from Malaga to Almería, winding high above the coastline in the dizziness of mountains and light for over a hundred miles, well deserves its appellation of *Costa del Sol*. Through Almuñecar, Motril, la Rábita, its constant beauty is never wearisome. Not only did the relief perpetually force its engineers to build the road in a series of bends, revealing fresh vistas at every turn, but Nature herself has seen to it that the effects of light, sea and land are continually varied. The brilliance of the landscape is such that it is not so much blue as golden, and the fragrance of the earth mingles with that of the Mediterranean. The *Costa del Sol* is truly the embodiment of perfect natural beauty.

**18–19
PEACEFUL
HARBOURS**

Spanish mariners linked Spain to the Indies, sailing in galleons laden with gold, often becalmed in the Atlantic waiting for a puff of wind to fill their sails. Such ships were a constant prey for the English fleet and Berber pirates. Those heroic days of seafaring are succeeded today only by the humble though picturesque everyday scenes of the Spanish fishing trade. But why waste regrets upon the sagas of the past? The pictures which follow are of happy boats without a history.

**18
TOSSÁ DE MAR**

The port of Tossá de Mar is situated between the French frontier and Barcelona, on the Costa Brava, where splendour of sea and mountain alternates, with sudden vistas of incomparable beauty. In this natural creek the lines of relief, boats and sea compose a graphic poem, every line converging on some mysterious centre.

**19
SAN CARLOS DE
LA RÁPITA**

At San Carlos de la Rápita, a little to the south of Amposta, a small, spruce craft, its sails whiter than the whitewashed houses past which it sails, seems to have embarked upon a calm and endless voyage on the lake of time, taking with it happiness and beauty.

The town of Casarabonela is midway between Malaga and Ronda as the crow flies, in a too-little-known region comprising the *hoya* or trough of Malaga and the *serranía* of Ronda (see note on Plate 23). The great villages in their splendid mountain settings seem to have remained untouched by modern life. The peacefulness of such scenes is unforgettable. The little town steeped in the tranquil sleep of countless centuries, seeming under the protection of the mountains, the heavy-laden mules and donkeys—the anachronism of such a life may astonish us, but we cannot remain impervious to its charm.

20

CASARABONELA IN THE PROVINCE OF MALAGA

Just over twenty-five miles west of Seville, Carmona stands in the centre of a fertile stretch of country. A number of its buildings remind us of Seville itself: the tower of San Pedro recalls the *Giralda* and Santa María the cathedral. The town possesses many fine churches, gateways and a Roman cemetery. A subtle Moorish atmosphere still pervades it. Yet, disregarding all this beauty, let us look for a moment just at this study in stone, wings and light, capturing in a moment's brief delight the snowy whiteness of three storks taking flight in the Andalusian sun.

21

STORKS AT CARMONA

It matters little whether these three well-to-do peasants, come to market to buy or sell their animals, are seen here full-face, back view or in profile; they allow us to visualize the downward trek from the smaller towns and villages to the great market towns on sale days. Every path and roadway bears a stream of men in black smocks and trousers, with hats or berets on their heads; the women's faces are expressionless from the brightness of the light; the animals seem heedless of the fate awaiting them and of the long road which lies ahead. An unending procession wends its way into the town to mill about its centre, accompanied by the extraordinary murmur made by the trampling of innumerable feet on earth and stone. Around the market ground itself, the crowd becomes an inextricable tangle and a curious clamour is heard, rising, falling and rising again, a medley of the intermittent noises of the animals and the incomprehensible shouting of the men. The *guardias* attempt in vain to introduce some order into a chaos without which the scene would lose all its charm.

Just outside the town, a few peasants, their business settled, linger for a pleasant exchange of conversation, or merely to await the closing of a day which has supplied a welcome break in the monotony of their existence. It is as though through the eyes of these men, fixed on the distant hurly-burly of the town, Spain itself—the strong and healthy peasant Spain of tradition—were engaged in contemplating its own image.

22

THE LIVESTOCK MARKET AT CORDOVA

**23
RONDA,
TOWN GATE**

Ronda lies in the centre of the *serranía*, a vast region of Andalusia forming a ring of mountains stretching for over twenty miles. The steepness of the slopes explains how it came about that the reconquest was here fraught with so much difficulty—Ronda falling only a few years before Granada itself—and why brigandage survived until well into the nineteenth century. Today, Ronda has preserved undiminished the prestige it owes not only to the surrounding countryside but also to its own incomparable situation. The *Tajo*, a sheer ravine nearly 500 feet in depth, separates the two halves of the town, providing a spectacularly plunging view. All around extends the calm expanse of the Andalusian countryside. The city gates might well bear an inscription running something like the following: 'Enter not in haste, O traveller, for the surprise of my precipice and the peacefulness of my landscape will last as long as earth itself.'

**24
THE VALLEY OF
THE RÍO TORMES**

This region of Spain is traditionally but inaccurately described as uniformly dry, whereas in fact the merest puddle produces moss, the smallest pool a clump of trees, while a stream bedecks the landscape in a thousand different shades of green. The valley of the Río Tormes, on which lies Salamanca, shows clearly what hidden reserves of delight can be conjured up by water. Its charm is composed from few elements: on every side rise the plateaux of León; the river bed itself is almost dry. Yet the simplicity of its beauty is a perfect expression of a calm and smiling nature, reaching a peak of poignant tenderness in those few brief moments when night still hesitates to engulf the twilight zones which the sun consents to yield as it sinks on the horizon. All its colours are then transmuted into tones of grey, soon to turn to black before the first stars begin to sparkle in the sky.

**25
PEASANTS ON
HORSEBACK
IN THE
LEÓN REGION**

These hooded horsemen—like monks evicted from their monastery by some war or revolution, or shepherds driven by storm from an already windswept landscape—are simply Spanish peasants going about their daily lives.
But their faces—earthy, obstinate and loyal—and their heavy cloaks, stained with dust of ages and of heavy labour, remind us of the monks of Zurbarán.

Plates 1-25

I

4

5

3

7

20

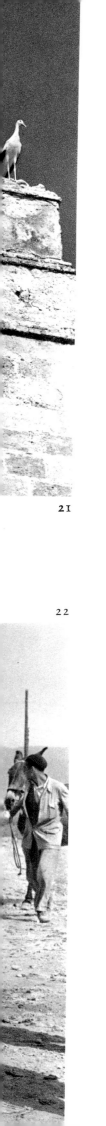

21

22

23

The Spanish Sun

Spain—an immensity of mountain chains and plateaux where burn ceaselessly new suns and birds of fire.

J. M.

MIDDAY. Prostrate, the country lies devoid of life—desiccated and consumed as though by fire. The meagre river crawls upon its way, the wind is sleeping. On road and pathway not a shadow falls, for the sun beats down directly on the great trees on either hand. Faced with such a landscape, we can see why Spanish painters have always been so loath to use transitional shades of colour. Here all colour is inflamed by sunlight and delicate, intermediate shades are crowded out. This image of a sun-struck land is what the traveller has come to Spain to find, a picture that varies with the individual character of the different regions: here the light falls steeply on Castilian grey of house and rock; there it makes the *huertas* blossom or fills with sweetness the Levantine palm groves; or, again, it bursts upon the whitewashed walls and olive-dotted lands of Andalusia.

But do such pictures, though apparently justifying Spain's reputation, really convey a true reflection? Probably not, for they by no means exhaust the manifold originality of the country. The Basque Provinces, the Asturias, Galicia, the northern coast reveal another and quite different poetic charm, that of the Atlantic, with its swiftly-changing climate: its rain, its mists, its greenery, its deep forests, the sea which invades the sand dunes in the *rias* of Galicia, compose tranquil colour symphonies of water, tree and wave in an infinitely ranging scale of blues and greens.

The truth of the matter is that while the sun is not the whole of Spain, without it, Spain is inconceivable. And there is an element of mystery about it that is all-important: the sun of Spain is not as any other sun; it is a firebird, sometimes single, sometimes a host, sometimes radiant and consuming as in Andalusia, sometimes spreading its vast wings in order to prolong the subtle play of light and shade. In Andalusia, this imperious bird bathes the Moorish buildings in a bloom of light.

In Seville, the courtyard which once stood before the mosque now leads to the cathedral: but among the branches of the orange trees the fruits still shine like tiny golden balls, and the gentle, almost imperceptible breeze, of morning, noon or twilight, sets the shady softness of their foliage atremble—with a tenuous hopefulness, with ardent joy or with a universal melancholy. Nearby, the *Giralda* stretches the soft finger of its shade towards the silent, heat-stricken city. With the Alcázar begins the almost disquieting peace of Moorish palaces in which the sun, reflected by *azulejos*, cupola and fountains, mingles with the scarcely stirring air.

Cordova, like an Arab queen, secret and withdrawn, silent among her snow-white palaces, has enticed into her mosque the bird of day; down the long avenues of shade it wings, suddenly to imprint upon column or cupola the light badge of its golden pinions. We behold a forest of stone and marble, of sparkling fire and captive firmament: while a myriad bright or muted shafts seem to culminate in the fluttering wings of innumerable red or russet birds beating against the arches in an effort to escape.

The secrecy of Cordova is matched by the radiance of Granada. Whether the morning sun breaks into its sleep with a flash of azure wings, or at evening leaves it suffused in rosy light, this fantastic city is instinct with poetry.

But the sight of those countless bright warriors revealed by the morning sun upon the high battlements of the Alhambra cannot be conveyed in words. Here the sun-bird has arrayed itself in rare feathers compounded of light and shadow. In the palace courtyards, which our imagination still peoples with courtly Moorish knights, pools and fountains mirror some splendid patch of sky, while hieratic lions offer their backs to the warming light, as for centuries past. In the gardens of the Generalife, the sun becomes a song-bird, conjured from fountain, marble and greenery; and, when evening shadows lengthen, it lingers on, wings growing still, to prolong the mystery of twilight.

Even outside the walls of the Alhambra, in the city stretching at its foot, the sun confers on beings and objects a degree of poetry unattainable without its aid. Federico García Lorca, writing to Ana María Dali, observed that in Granada the Mediterranean vegetation shone 'with all the delicacy of its fantastic range of greys', and, in a spirit of gentle mockery, spoke of the way the light transforms young maidens into sunflowers or even into useless chattering birds, bestowing on each one of their daily occupations a different hue. 'When it is fine, the young ladies of Granada go up into their white-washed *miradores* wishing to see the mountains and not the sea. The blonde ones take up their positions in the sun, the dark ones prefer the shade. But those who have auburn hair remain indoors, contemplating their own image in the mirror, adjusting their great celluloid combs. In the afternoon, attired in diaphanous or silken dresses they go walking by the flashing fountains, there to experience the time-honoured torture of the rose and the melancholy pangs of love. After which they stuff themselves with sweets and cakes in a shop which should bear the name "Paris de France" but which, in fact, is called "The Aviary".'

Finally, throughout the length and breadth of Andalusia, in every patio from the most famous to the humblest, the iron trellises and sprays of greenery, shot through by shafts of light, seem to form a phantom cage imprisoning a flock of fluttering sparrows of dappling light and shade.

These blue-grey sparrows, nesting in the churches, monasteries and palaces of Castile and León, appear as so many mysterious stars, now shining, now invisible.

Flushing to red the yellow stones of Salamanca, nestling in the shells of the *Casa de las conchas*, they shed an almost Roman light upon the towers and domes of its two cathedrals and on the *Clerecía*, or Jesuit church. They also come to rest under the vast and shadowy porch which stands before the church of the Monastery of San Estebán.

In Avila, the light is as cold as spiritual standards are exacting, but on occasion the sunbirds' path crosses that of the storks, those harbingers of spring. At Valladolid, these same birds weave constantly between the twisted columns of the patio of the Colegio de San Gregorio, rejuvenating for a moment the old façade of San Pablo, a remarkable reredos wearing the patina conferred upon it by the centuries.

At Burgos, the sun assumes a heroic rôle and the air is filled with the sudden glint of steel, forged by the birds of war. At Toledo, all is ardour, a very conflagration of heart and heaven, for though the imperial city now reclines upon the broken eagles' wings of its former glory, it is held in thrall by the fiery breath of the firmament.

Each town or village is watched over by a guardian bird, which according to the day and hour, renders it pleasing, ravishing or disquieting. In the cathedrals this column is softly luminous, but not its neighbour. On one altar screen the gold is filled with song, for the doves are playing; from another they have already fled, leaving it to dust, to sadness and obscurity. From some cupola, some rose window—imposing or insignificant—a falling shaft of sunlight restores the touch of youth to the wrought maturity of the grilles. In the cloisters the play of light and shade, the flutter of white and grey wings, is inseparable from the freshness of the fountains and the swaying of the branches. Hour after hour the murmur of the water in the ritual fountain for the monks' ablutions accompanies the motion of the sun.

In the towns the sun becomes a street-bird, filling the streets with blinding heat, transforming the chalk-white of the houses into snowy torches. From dawn till dusk it pays court to the four corners of the public square: men, women and children, sitting in shade cast by jutting walls sharply silhouetted by the sky, observe the beating of its wings; several times a day they change their location, taking with them their gossip, their embroidery and their games. When at last the Firebird itself goes to rest, the inhabitants, freed at least from its implacable thraldom, pour forth from the arcades of all the *plazas mayores*, from the patios and other shady corners; for now the shadows spread to engulf the entire city. This is the blessed hour of the *paseo*, the promenade, the apéritif, of endless conversation—until such time as the sky kindles the torches of the stars, humble torches that generate no heat and little light. The changing hours of day and night govern the coming and going of all these birds of light and shade. But there are others which the mind and hand of man, consciously or unconsciously, has created out of the obsessive image of the sun and the stars: arc, circle, disk, the star, the aurole, the halo—all have served the ends of art. The eye of the camera sees them as so many visual poems born of obsession with the sun.

Either blinded by light, or sun-dappled, or drowsing in the shade, the face of Spain is for ever subject to the sun's alternating torture, flattery or tender care: it is a face whose features we must ceaselessly explore in our search for its essential beauty, and even more, the secrets it holds.

The whole region of Huelva is closely associated with the discovery of the Americas. In 1492 and 1493, Palos saw the departure and return of Christopher Columbus. A few miles away, the Franciscan monastery of La Rábida, standing on a hillside at the confluence of the Odiel and the Río Tinto, reminds us that here Prior Juan Pérez de Marchena first extended to Columbus his encouragement and help. The church, a combination of gothic and *mudéjar*, dates from the fourteenth century. The cloister, or patio, built a century later, has been restored in *mudéjar* style. The monastery itself is now a national monument. *Alicatado* is a variety of ceramic work, of Moslem origin and peculiar to Andalusia; it is made up of a mosaic of tiny pieces, each of a single colour, forming a pattern which, of course, may be polychrome. The design illustrated consists of star-shaped polygons. The technique of *alicatado* attained perfection as early as the end of the thirteenth century. It seems practically impossible to distinguish work executed in a Granada still under Moslem rule from that executed during the same period—during the thirteenth or fourteenth centuries—by Moors or Christians in reconquered Andalusia (Seville was recaptured in 1248 and Huelva in 1257). The *alicatados* in the Alhambra in Granada are particularly fine—notably in the *Torre de las Damas*, the *Sala de Comares*, the *Torre de la Cautiva*, the *Sala de las Dos Hermanas*, and the *Mirador de Daraxa*.

26
Alicatado: patio in the
monastery of La Rábida

In Baghdad in the year 750 the Omayyads were massacred and overthrown by the Abbasids. A prince of the conquered dynasty, named Abd-ar-Rahman, succeeded in reaching Africa and subsequently Moslem Spain. Here, in 756, he proclaimed himself an independent Emir. Setting up his capital at Cordova, he was destined to make an important contribution to the spread of a magnificent Islamic civilization in the

27–30
CORDOVA
CATHEDRAL
(formerly the Great
Mosque)

29
Suite of arched bays

27
Cupola of the *kebla* or ante-
chamber to the *mihrab*

28
Decorated archways with
multifoil arches

30
Decorated archways near
the *mihrab*

Iberian peninsula. In 785, Abd-ar-Rahman I, seeking to reproduce the splendours of
the Orient and to demonstrate his power, undertook the construction of the Great
Mosque. The original building, which was extended by Hisham I, comprised first nine,
then eleven naves. These were extended again in a southerly direction in 833 and 848
by Abd-ar-Rahman II. In this part of the mosque (see Plate 29) the columns are arranged in rows, using the remains of former Roman or Visigothic monuments, and they
and the double superposed arches, with their black and white voussoirs, compose almost
unlimited perspectives. The architects doubtless had in mind the monuments of Syria
and Egypt, as well as those of classic times still extant on Spanish soil, such as the
aqueduct of *Los Milagros* at Mérida. Al-Hakam II again prolonged the naves in a
southerly direction (961–966), constructing the new portion which contains the *mihrab*
and its ante-room, or *kebla* (Plates 27, 28 and 30). The decoration here is reminiscent
of Syrian or Sassanid art; sumptuous in conception, with a profusion of multifoil
arches, marble, stucco and mosaics. The ribbed cupolas give an unforgettable impression of soaring opulence. Finally, between 987 and 990, a further eight naves were
added, this time on the eastern side and running the whole length of the existing
mosque. After the Reconquest, the mosque was transformed into a cathedral, when the
entrance from the nave on to the *Patio de los Naranjos* was blocked up. In the course of
the sixteenth century a *coro* and a *capilla mayor* were built in the very heart of the old
mosque, destroying the internal harmony of a whole section of its architecture. In spite
of this, thanks to its spaciousness, its decoration, and its state of preservation, the Great
Mosque of Cordova remains not only (together with the Alhambra in Granada) the
most beautiful monument left by Islam on Spanish soil, but one of the most remarkable
in the whole of Islamic civilization. Historians, archaeologists and poets alike can all
find satisfaction in the infinite avenues of marble, stucco and mosaic. It is no longer a
mosque, nor yet truly a cathedral. The Crescent has been banished, but the Cross has
never been truly planted in its soul. Poetry and knowledge alone can restore it to its
full beauty.

31
TOLEDO: SANTA
MARÍA LA
BLANCA

The Jews occupied a place of prime importance in medieval Toledo, contributing
greatly to its prosperity and fame, not only as merchants and bankers, but as astrono-
mers and philosophers too. The Jewish quarter extended to the south-west of the city.
Of all the synagogues built there in the Middle Ages, only two remain: the *Tránsito*
and *Santa María la Blanca*, both converted into Christian churches.
As a result of a fire which occurred in about the year 1250 Santa María la Blanca under-
went a complete restoration, probably at some time during the second half of the
thirteenth century. The building has five parallel naves separated by horse-shoe-
shaped arches, the central nave being higher and wider than the others. The pillars are

decorated at the base with painted ceramic tiles (*azulejos*) and crowned at the top with *yeserías*—prodigiously sculpted decorative plaster motifs, resembling capitals. Motifs similar in style, and executed in the same material, decorate the walls above the arches. Santa María la Blanca is an example of the work of local Toledan artisans, notably in the brickwork, but it also bears shining testimony to Islamic influences from Andalusia. In Spain, the term *mudéjar* is applied to art designed for Christians or Jews—that is, for non-Moslems—but which employs Islamic motifs, mingling them with those of Western Christendom. Toledo is one of the towns where this art was markedly successful.

Three plateresque chapels have been added to the original synagogue, reminding us of the sometimes conflicting, sometimes harmonious, but always exciting sequence of styles, peoples and religions, both here and elsewhere in Toledo.

After the Reconquest, the Kings of Castile took over the Alcázar of the Moslem rulers of Seville for their residence, enriching it in the traditions of Hispano-Moorish art. Pedro I made the Alcázar his favourite residence and commissioned much magnificent work.

The walls of the *Sala des Ambacadores* are covered with *azulejos* and plaster motifs. Round the upper portion of the walls runs a frieze of portraits of the royal house of Castile. The cupola rests on gilded squinches in the shape of stalactites: the cupola itself is in *artesonado*, that is, it is composed of sunken panels of gilded and painted wood. At the summit are to be distinguished the lions and castles symbolic of León and Castile. It is as though Moslem Spain had sought to revenge itself upon the conquering Christian kings by the very excellence of its art.

32
THE ALCÁZAR
OF SEVILLE:
cupola of the *Sala des
Ambacadores*

When most of Andalusia had fallen to the Kingdom of Castile, the Nasrides dynasty, founded in 1278 by Ibd-el-Ahmar, selected Granada as the capital of an independent state—a state destined to survive until the capture of Granada itself by the Catholic sovereigns in 1492. Granada became in addition a new centre of Moslem art and culture, destined to take the place of Cordova and Seville.

Within the precincts of the Alhambra—flanked by towers and high walls, its golden, sun-lit stones seeming to float on the horizon above the city—we must distinguish between the *Alcazaba*, or fortress, dating back to the early reigns of the dynasty, and the *Casa Reál*, a series of palaces constructed, without any preconceived plan, by Yusuf I (1333–1354) and Mohamed V (1354–1391). These two kings were responsible for the construction of the most famous halls and courtyards of the Alhambra. After the fall of Granada, the Catholic sovereigns lived for a time in the Alhambra. Considerable work

33, 34, 36–38
THE POETRY OF
WESTERN
ISLAMIC ART:
THE ALHAMBRA
AND THE
GENERALIFE OF
GRANADA

was put in hand by Charles V, who entrusted to Machuca the construction of a new Palace (Plates 150–151). Within these walls history and legend, drama and passion, intrigue and bloodshed, memories of poets and of writers have merged with the very spirit of the stones, so that our minds are filled with thoughts of the Abencerrages, the fall of Boabdil, of Chateaubriand and Washington Irving. Recollections no sooner evoked than forgotten, for the Alhambra possesses the rare quality of raising memories without allowing them to become obsessive. To the Alhambra, the adulation of an admirer is simply one more flower to add to its already copious bouquet. Outside the precincts, the Moorish kings constructed a number of minor palaces and gardens, the better to appreciate both view and solitude. The Generalife is one such residence which time has not destroyed.

33
THE ALHAMBRA,
GRANADA:
Court of the Lions

Around the *Patio de los Leones* stood the private apartments of the Moorish sovereigns: this part of the Alhambra was built by Mohamed V. The patio is flanked by four galleries leading to four halls: the Hall of the Kings, the *Mocarabes*, the *Dos Hermanas*— its name derives from two marble slabs as like one another as two sisters—and the *Abencerrages*. Original features of the court are the square temples standing at the centre of the shorter sides, the richness of form and ornament, the subtlety of the decoration and the grace of the marble fountain; these are in contrast with the more primitive forms of the lions which flank the fountain. The almost archaic style of these beasts does much to save the patio from a certain excess of opulence and refinement.

34
GRANADA: the
Patio de la Acequia in the
Generalife

The Generalife has always been confined to few buildings, and these on a small scale. It is composed essentially of small courtyards and buildings, interspersed with gardens. These separate, walled and shady gardens, fresh, fragrant and peaceful, are divided again within, with no attempt at creating long vistas. The heart and mind delight in their cunningly contrived intricacy.

The *Patio de la Acequia* is closed on its northern and southern sides by two small porticoed pavilions, while the remaining sides are bounded by plain walls. Here all is a profusion of delicate perfumes, rustling leaves and murmuring fountains. A nearby *mirador* provides the dazzling surprise of a magnificent vista over the Alhambra with its complex network of architecture and gardens.

On the heights of Malaga, above the laughing, fragrant town, and the harbour where the sirens of departing boats wail their invitation to departure, stands the *Alcazaba*, embodying many centuries rich in history. For its original construction the Moors made use of a former Roman fortress. This remarkable palace has now been restored, and possesses a number of fine semicircular and horse-shoe arches. It abuts on the *Gibralfaro* castle, another fourteenth-century Moorish building, also with an interesting arched portal, decorated in brickwork.

35
MALAGA: doorway
between the *Alcazaba*
and the *Gibralfaro*

The *Patio de Comares* was completed by Mohamed V in about the year 1369. It is rectangular in shape; at one end stands a gallery formed by seven semicircular arches, supported by marble pillars, and leading to a sumptuous reception room and a tower of the same name. The central arch, higher than the others, breaks the regularity of line. Contrasting with this gallery, the walls on the longer sides of the rectangle are pierced by relatively few doors and windows. The still waters of the pool, the decoration of the archways, the tiling of the walls and the green hedges all compose a single, subtle harmony. The Court of the Myrtles evokes the music of a violin—a strain so perfect that it must always be on the point of breaking off, yet which flows on unfailingly.

The *Patio de Daraxa* is planted with laurel and with cypress and enriched by a marble fountain, conveying an exquisitely poetic atmosphere. It is surrounded on all sides by the apartments built by Charles V. Today a walled garden, full of romantic charm, in Moslem days it was a favourite vantage point from which to contemplate the surrounding countryside.

The *Torre de las Damas* was constructed towards the end of the thirteenth or in the early part of the fourteenth century. On its garden side, facing the interior of the Alhambra, stands a portico of remarkable grace and delicacy. The most demanding traveller will find his expectations exceeded by tower and *mirador*, the arches mirrored in the water, the surrounding hedges and trees. Here, in miniature, is all that he is seeking: the beauty of a particular type of art, nature as an enchanting accomplice, and all the joy of sunlight mingled with the song of birds.

39
AVILA: Church of San Vicente. Tomb of San Vicente and his sisters

The Church of San Vicente, begun in romanesque and continued in gothic style, was raised outside the city walls on the site where the Saint and his two sisters were martyred in the fourth century. Their tomb consists of a twelfth-century sarcophagus, carved with moving scenes from the story of their martyrdom. This sarcophagus rests on pillars under a kind of gothic canopy carved in stone.

On the west side of the church an impressive doorway is decorated with foliage motifs and statues of the saints; the south doorway portrays an Annunciation. The Church of San Vicente is interesting both for its architecture, which marks the beginnings of gothic art in Castile, and for its sculpture, which is reminiscent of that of the *Cámara santa* of Oviedo or of the *Portico de la Gloria* of St James of Compostela.

40
BARCELONA: Cloister of the Church of San Pablo del Campo

This romanesque church dates from the twelfth century, but was certainly founded some time before: two capitals dating from the seventh and eighth centuries were re-employed in the construction of the porch. The cloister was built in the thirteenth century: on the capitals, which rest on twin pillars supporting triple arches, are carved monsters, battle scenes and plant motifs. The name *San Pablo del Campo* derives from the church's original location in the cultivated stretch of country between Barcelona and Montjuich. Today this name is in striking contrast to the urban activity by which the church is surrounded. Yet the fresh green foliage and mellowness of the cloister continue to create an atmosphere of medieval peacefulness.

41
SEGOVIA: the cathedral vaulting

Seen from the outside, the cathedral of Segovia is a splendid vision of soaring russet stone; inside, this soaring effect is maintained, though with greater subtlety. It seems that this impression owes its impact to the fact that the cathedral, begun in 1525, represents, like the new cathedral of Salamanca, the survival of gothic into the fifteenth century—a gothic at once delicate and majestic, florid and sober. The pattern of the vaulting illustrated shows these same qualities. The architects were Juan Gil de Hontañón and his son Rodrigo.

42
THE PALM GROVES OF ELCHE

Irrigation has made it possible for Elche to boast what are undoubtedly the most extensive palm groves in Europe. Some of the palms are carefully bandaged to protect them from the light, so that their fronds remain white, and may be used for certain ceremonies peculiar to Holy Week. The town also owes a part of its fame to the discovery of a magnificent Iberian sculpture, the *Lady of Elche*, formerly in Louvre, and now in the Prado.

After the reconquest of Seville Ferdinand III established Christian worship in the Great Mosque of the city. But with the passage of time, and following upon a series of earthquakes, it became necessary early in the fifteenth century to build a new cathedral. This decision was reached on 8th July 1401, amid great enthusiasm, by the members of the cathedral chapter—who even offered to forgo their own stipends if necessary. Work began in 1402 and ended on 10th November 1506. The dome collapsed on 28th December 1511, whereupon the architect of the cathedral of Segovia, Juan Gil de Hontañón, was called in to direct the subsequent restoration.

Beneath the powerful vaults, even more florid than those of Segovia, we may find ourselves repeating the words of Luis de Peraza, who during the sixteenth century addressed to the city of Seville the following lines:

> Tienes un templo de gran maravilla,
> entierro de reyes y gran clerecía,
> que en letras y fe y gran armonía
> nos hace veamos ser Roma Sevilla.
>
> *You have a church of great splendour,*
> *a sepulchre for kings and great churchmen,*
> *who, by letters, faith and deep concord*
> *make Seville a second Rome for us.*

43
SEVILLE:
the cathedral vaulting

The silk market in Valencia was built by the architect Pedro Compte between 1483 and 1498. The vault rests on eight spiral columns and corresponding wall pillars; the delicacy of the ribbing and the soaring movement of the columns call to mind a palm grove. This market is reminiscent of a similar architectural triumph, the market of Palma de Mallorca, designed by Guillermo Sagrera (1426–1466), which served as an inspiration to Pedro Compte.

The building's beauty delights us all the more for its parallel with natural beauty. To the historian it serves as a reminder of the opulence and prosperity of Valencia and the surrounding region. This market is both a masterpiece of Levantine gothic and a testimony to the importance of Valencia in the Mediterranean world of the fifteenth century.

44
VALENCIA:
Lonja de la Seda

Building of Burgos Cathedral was begun in about the year 1120 by Bishop Mauricio, on the model of Bourges, Le Mans and Coutances, and continued by Maître Henri; the cathedral was ornamented by sculpture reminiscent of French gothic tympanums and portals. In the course of the fifteenth and sixteenth centuries it was further enriched by three architects from the Rhineland: Juan, Simon and Francisco de Colonia. Behind

45
BURGOS
CATHEDRAL:
Capilla del Condestable

the *Capilla mayor*, in the centre of the ambulatory, Simon added, some time between 1485 and 1490, the Chapel of Don Pedro Hernández de Velasco, Constable of Castile. The tombs of the Constable and his wife which lie within this chapel are among the most moving examples of Spanish funerary sculpture.

The cupola is formed by two complementary eight-point stars, the lesser set within the greater. The high, balustraded windows surmounted by stone-fringed arches appear not so much to be supporting the cupola as to be thrusting it upwards, towards the sunlight which streams ceaselessly down from its centre.

46–47
VALLADOLID:
Court of the *Colegio de San Gregorio*

The college of San Gregorio was founded in 1487 by Fray Alonso de Burgos, Bishop of Palencia, and the building was constructed during the years 1488 to 1496. Its façade, which is related to certain Manueline works of Portuguese art, and its richly decorated *patio*, in which the gothic tradition merges with memories of *mudéjar*, are among the finest architectural works of the reign of the Catholic sovereigns.

The college contains the national museum of sculpture, which is remarkably well arranged. Here we find the *Saint Sebastián* (Plate 128) and *Sacrifice of Isaac* by Alfonso Berruguete (1488–1561), an *Entombment* by Juan de Juni (1506?–1577), a *Baptism of Christ*, a *Saint Teresa*, and among the *pasos* or processional figures, the *Virgin of Compassion* by Gregorio Fernández (1566?–1636).

48
BURGOS: Church of San Nicolas, detail of the high altar reredos

While the true miracle of Burgos is its cathedral, one of its chief charms lies in its many delightful churches. Behind the high altar of the church of San Nicolas (fifteenth century) is a polychrome alabaster reredos completed by Francisco de Colonia in 1505. In the lower section, under a flattened arch, several small canopies shelter a series of scenes from the life of St Nicholas. The Saint is represented in the centre by a statue which is of an earlier date than the remainder of the work. The upper portion is perhaps the more remarkable: the centre is occupied by a *Coronation of the Virgin*, while all around radiate lines of angels, surrounding the Mother of God in a vast halo, with wave upon wave of heads, wings and robes.

49
BARCELONA:
chandelier in the Palace of the *Diputación General*

The dome which supports this chandelier plays the rôle of firmament: its pictures supply a universe of characters and colours. Unlighted, the chandelier is like some monster poised menacingly above our heads: enormous and heavy with metal and crystal. But when ablaze with countless lights, it is transfigured into a sun, the very heart of a Creation quickening to life and light. This chandelier hangs in the *Salon de San Jorge*, which is decorated with modern paintings.

The palace of the *Diputación General* forms a single architectural unit with the neighbouring *Audiencia*; this was constructed during the fifteenth and sixteenth centuries, and is famous for its gothic courtyard, its *Patio de los Naranjos*, the chapel of San Jorge and the relief of this saint executed by Father Johan in 1418.

Toledo cathedral, begun in 1225, belongs to the line of gothic cathedrals culminating in the magnificent creations of Notre-Dame in Paris and Saint Etienne in Bourges. In the course of several centuries of construction it was enriched by the addition of chapels, altar screens and tombs—a remarkable profusion of works of art and of Christian fervour. It combines a radiant majesty with the constant surprises of a wealth of decorative detail added by succeeding generations. In the eighteenth century, an Archbishop of the city, Don Diego de Astorgo y Cespedes, was shocked to find that nothing recalled to worshippers passing through the ambulatory the presence of the Eucharist at the high altar in the background. The result was the *Transparente* executed by Narciso Tomé between 1721 and 1732. The artist has surrounded the two main motifs with a veritable legion of angels. At the top he has portrayed the Last Supper and, half-way down, a radiant sun, directing eye and mind towards the Host. The intrusion of this *Transparente* into a gothic edifice was long considered scandalous. Now, however, the work is regarded as one of the most remarkable examples of Spanish baroque, and admirable for the skill and symbolism of the concept, the vigour of its grouping and the poetry of its angel- and cloud-filled universe.

50
TOLEDO
CATHEDRAL:
the *Transparente*

The work of Antonio Gaudi is inspired by an almost lyrical impulse of form and decoration. It is remarkable alike for the skill and logic of its construction and for its exuberance and sensitivity. Ever since the Exhibition of 1888 the architecture of Barcelona has borne the stamp of his masterly hand. To him it owes the *Casa Güell* of 1885, the *Parque Público*, the *Casa Millá* of 1910, and the church of the *Sagrada Familia*. The gothic elements of the *Sagrada Familia* are only one aspect of the church and should not be allowed to conceal the dynamic magnitude of the over-all conception, apparent despite its unfinished state. Gaudi died prematurely in 1926. He cannot be typed according to any one monument or style, or even according to the Barcelona of a particular period; he must be studied in the wider context of European 'art nouveau' of the late nineteenth and early twentieth centuries.

51
BARCELONA:
church of the *Sagrada Familia*

52
SALAMANCA:
Casa de las Conchas

Built for Dr Don Rodrigo Arias Maldonado in the late fifteenth or early sixteenth century, at the time when the medieval castle was beginning to give way to the residential palace, the *Casa de las Conchas* has been aptly described by F. Chueca as 'an incomparable mixture of gothic naturalism, *mudéjar* and the Renaissance'. The façade is decorated with the Maldonado arms, the *fleur de Lys*, and strewn with the cockle shells (*conchas*) of the Benavente family to which Don Rodrigo was related. The combination of sturdy architecture and the virile poetry of heraldic emblems, together with the charm of its patio, make the *Casa de las Conchas* one of the most remarkable palaces in the whole of Spain.

53–61
PATTERNS OF
LIGHT AND
SHADE

Every time we seek rest and refreshment in some shady corner, the sun discovers our intention and overwhelms us with its light. When, on the other hand, we seek the light, the mocking sun greets us with a wall of shadow. This sport, pursued with ceaseless coquetry by the Spanish sun on man and object, has been captured by the camera both in famous street and hidden corner, each with its distinctive charm.

53
SEVILLE: a patio in the
Barrio de Santa Cruz

The Santa Cruz quarter consists of an unforgettable network of narrow streets and tiny squares. Whitewashed walls lead us towards fountains, whence rise the joyous songs of innumerable birds. Shaded by the overhanging boughs of orange blossom, children are at play. From time to time, through some open doorway, we have the good fortune to catch a glimpse of an interior, the patio with its wrought-iron grilles, its *azulejos*, its plants and its arches—a small oasis of refreshment touched with a delicate intimacy which we could wish to enjoy less fleetingly.

54
SEVILLE
CATHEDRAL:
Patio de los Naranjos

The *Patio de los Naranjos*, lying on the northern side of the cathedral of Seville, is the purification court of the mosque which once occupied the site of the present building, and which itself replaced an earlier Visigoth cathedral. The circular basin of the fountain in the centre of the patio is said to have come from this original cathedral. Thus three eras, three civilizations, are merged in perfect harmony in the sun of Seville, suffused by the enchanting fragrance of the orange blossom.

Without ever completely losing its fortress-like appearance, the Moorish *Alcázar* of Madrid was gradually transformed into a palace by the Habsburg kings. After it had been destroyed by fire at Christmas, 1734, Philip V—grandson of Louis XIV married to Elizabeth Farnese of the House of Parma—called upon the services of Juvara, the most celebrated Italian architect of the day. But Juvara died before he could complete the work of reconstruction. His plans, however, were adopted with modifications by his pupil Sachetti, who built the present palace (1737–1764). The West front of the main building, on the edge of the steep slope dominating the valley of the Manzanares, is remarkably spacious in design. To the south, the Parade Ground (*Plaza de Armas*) conveys a noble and harmonious impression. The gallery, seen here on the right, is a nineteenth-century addition.

55
ROYAL PALACE
OF MADRID:
the *Plaza de Armas*

The Jewish quarter of Cordova contains a synagogue, which with *Santa María la Blanca* in Toledo is certainly the most famous in all Spain. The narrow, secret, twisting streets have an atmosphere very different from that of the Sevillian *Barrio de Santa Cruz*: no longer intimate, refreshing and poetic, at once reserved and welcoming, but, on the contrary, conveying a constant sense of mystery, an enigma all the more extraordinary in that it persists even against the blinding whiteness of the walls, under the white-washed arcades, beneath the flower-decked windows. Cordova is a dark rose slowly surrendering to the visitor the fragrance of petals amassed and kept inviolate through the long years since the Moorish domination.

56
CORDOVA:
Barrio de la Judería

The *Pueblo*, or Spanish Village, built during the Exhibition of 1929, shows side by side models of a number of the most picturesque towns and districts of Spain. Navarre, the Levant, Andalusia and Castile are thus available, 'on the doorstep', so to speak, to the inhabitants of Barcelona.
But upon this synthesis of Spanish provinces the sun has not deigned to vary its effects: let us therefore snap our fingers at him and cross the sea to sample the shade and Mediterranean freshness of the Balearics.

57
BARCELONA:
the *Pueblo*

Beneath the sharp, geometrically pure line of these arches, protected from the sun, man can dream at leisure. His thoughts float as nonchalantly as the smoke from his cigarette, while on the ground before him lies a fishing net. This photograph has all the elements of a deliberate pictorial composition, but while its lines were determined by the

58
PALMA DE
MALLORCA:
arcades along the port

architect of the arcade, it depends for its life and variety on the light brought up sharp against its threshold like waves against the quayside.

59
SEVILLE:
terrace of a café near the
Capilla de San José

Here in the heart of Seville, near the narrow *Calle de las Sierpes*, protected by awnings from the sun in summer, is a typical Spanish tourist-season scene. A group of foreigners pauses for rest and refreshment and to send the inevitable postcards to their friends and relatives: 'This is to show you that in spite of the heat we really have come down as far as Andalusia.' Behind them the natives of Seville pursue some animated discussion which has no doubt been going on for some hours already, or at least for as long as that particular table has been in the shade. Only a few feet away sunlight floods the street, and a baroque façade affords a charming curving background. This is the *Capilla de San José*; its interior is one of the most richly ornamented sanctuaries of Seville (Plate 157).

60
SEVILLE:
the shadow of the *Giralda*

La Giralda is the minaret of a mosque long since replaced by the cathedral. Constructed at the end of the twelfth century, increased in height two centuries later, *La Giralda* is essential to any description of Seville. It has become the symbol of the town itself, and even when not in sight continues to offer the city the protection of its shadow!

61
PEASANT AT
TORRIJOS

Seen at Torrijos, a village some fifty miles south-west of Madrid, this peasant may serve to show once again how Spanish sun and earth have moulded the faces and the characters of the inhabitants of Spain. His is a face deeply carved by the sun into zones of light and shadow, the cast of the features accentuated by extremes of climate. His gaze, long accustomed to the sweep of wide horizons, is fixed upon the distance.

Plates 26-61

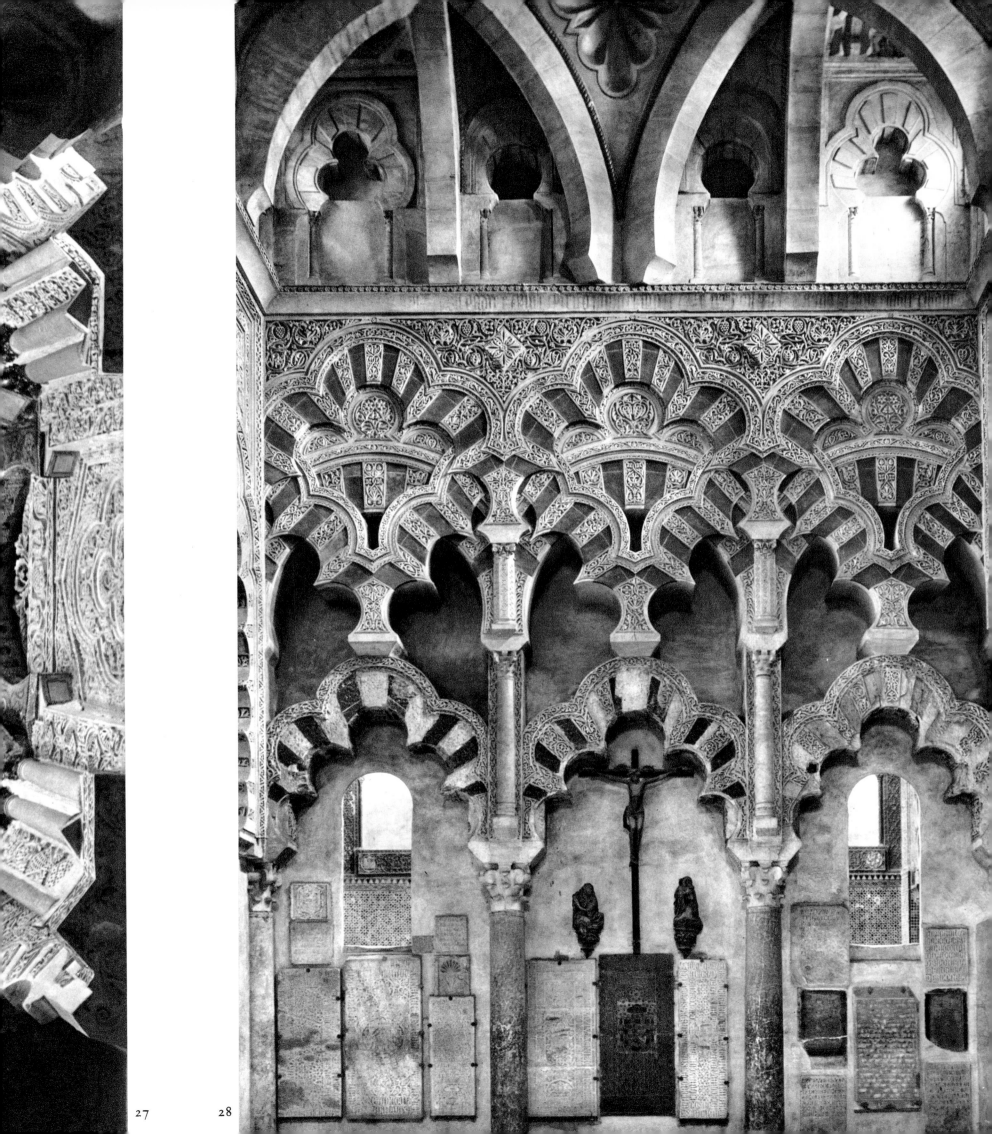

37

42

43

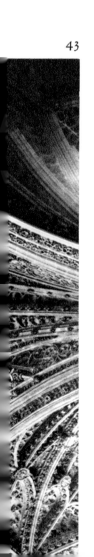

44

53

54

56

57

58

59

The Men and Cities of Spain

Muy despacio y como si no pudiese más,
de tanto que decía, ha dicho ella entonces:
'Si eres tû, si eres yo, abriré.'

Very slowly, as if she could manage no more—
so deeply moved was she—she said:
'If it's you, if it's me, I shall open.'

RAFAEL SÁNCHEZ MAZAS
La Vida nueva de Pedrito de Andía

IN THE COURSE OF SEVERAL DAYS of rapid travel the tourist usually builds up for himself a highly superficial, if not conventional picture of Spain, receiving a confused sequence of brilliant, highly coloured, but inevitably somewhat tendentious impressions. Castanets, toreadors ready for the kill, all the extravaganza of a Spanish Holy Week: a few phrases are sufficient to fill in the general picture, though it is tempting to prolong the list of 'Spanish' evocations. Dances which, according to the requirements of the hour or season, are conveniently labelled gipsy, Sevillian or Andalusian; rhythmically swaying hips; fiery glances; skirts which sweep and swirl like nightmare tops; *corridas* devoid of art, in which the bulls refuse to fight and the rashness of the matadors is matched only by their inexperience. And finally, the solemn moments of Holy Week itself transformed into a spectacle for the very tourists least likely to understand the religious feeling of a Mediterranean people. Alas, for the immutable dictates of the tourist trade! Since for the moment we are concerned only with the most obvious bait dangled before the eyes of the least discriminating tourist, let us add another feature or two. Why, for instance, attribute such exclusive importance to the *toros*, when football now represents so powerful a rival to the *corrida*? To see this for oneself one has only to watch the crowds issuing from the Madrid stadium after a match between two major teams. The rivalry of Madrid and Barcelona is now a permanent feature of modern Spanish life, and foreign triumphs by one or other of these teams is greeted as a new Lepanto!

How can we possibly describe with sufficient verve and irony the rôle of the telephone in the life of a great Spanish city? The telephone company is independent of the Post Office, and until quite recently, as in Madrid for example, local private calls were not charged for on an individual basis; as a result, once the subscription had been paid the instrument was in constant use. Even now, the price of a call is, to a foreigner, ridiculously low. Small wonder then that engaged couples are continually on the telephone, that young girls break off in the middle of a conversation to use their lipsticks, and that little servant girls, fresh from their native Andalusia, handle the instrument with remarkable dexterity, replying unabashedly to the calls of the young soldiers encountered in the Retiro in the course of their daily constitutional with the children of the house! In Spain, the very wires of progress hum with stanzas composed by loving but illiterate hearts.

In the city streets of Spain, and more particularly those of Madrid, Barcelona, Seville and Valencia, congestion, noise, exclamation, theatrical gesture and virtuosity in traffic-dodging reach an all-time record. In the smaller towns, towards evening the whole population descends into the streets, strolling to and fro, covering the same ground at least ten times over, so that the policeman's whistle, far from being directed at the errant motorist, is used exclusively to intimate to pedestrians the necessity of yielding at least an occasional passage to wheeled traffic!

But all these scenes compose a Spain whose features are easily discerned; we must search out the spirit behind the all-too-familiar face. Antonio Machado, while prophesying the birth of a new Spain, celebrated with teasing tenderness:

> *Spain of fanfares and of castanets,*
> *prison and sacristy*
> *devoted to the Virgin and the matador,*
> *of mocking spirit and serene soul,*
> *you will have your tomb and your day,*
> *your certain future and your poet.*

The wealth of popular Spanish song and folklore, the flamenco and Andalusian traditions, and in general, the atmosphere of southern Spain have often enough inspired poets and musicians. Albeniz has evoked in music *Corpus Christi in Seville*, *Triana* and *Albaïcin*. Manuel de Falla's *Amor Brujo* is based on an occult ritual: its subtitle 'Gipsy Scene in Andalusia' speaks for itself, while the titles of the various episodes, promising a music very close in inspiration to popular tradition—though remaining highly individual—are even more significant: *Song of Love's Grief, Dance of Terror, The Magic Circle, Song of the Jack O' Lantern, Dance of the Game of Love*. His *Nights in the Gardens of Spain*, in spite of certain technical affinities with Debussy, expresses ideas and themes native to Granada, Cordova and Andalusia.

The work of the doomed but unforgettable poet Federico García Lorca—not only his *Romancero Gitano* but also many other poems—springs from similar sources. Lorca is also the author of the *Lament for Ignacio Sánchez Mejías*, prince of matadors, who died in 1935 of a wound received during a *corrida*. This *Lament*, magnificently set to music by Maurice Ohana, shows the continuing importance of tauromachian art in contemporary Spain. It had already been the subject of famous engravings by Francisco Goya. Basically, such art celebrates the pitching of man's courage and skill against the terrifying brute force of the mindless beast: a ballet culminating always in the killing of the beast and often in the wounding of the man. The *corrida* is great only when its protagonist is a true champion of the ring. A very different emotion—nearer to dismay—is aroused when we come upon some old torero whom glory has eluded, but who still pursues with his companions his odyssey from ring to ring, decked in a spangled costume, earning his daily bread at the peril of his life. The bull-fight represents an essential facet of the Spanish temperament: love of danger and contempt for death.

Spanish Catholicism will strike many people—and not without reason—as unusual, to say the least. With varying degrees of discretion, the Church manages to occupy in Spain a place which may be judged too prominent, but which certainly serves to explain its rôle in the formation and history of the Spanish nation. Besides, there are more gradations and variations of opinion among the Spanish clergy than is commonly imagined. The ostentatious and almost oriental splendour of Holy Week celebrations expresses the genuine religious feeling of the Spanish people, instinctively inclined towards highly coloured spectacle and strong emotion. The same religious feeling finds expression in the popularity of the pilgrimage throughout the centuries: pilgrimage to Montserrat; to the monastery of Guadalupe; to the shrine of the Virgin of the Pillar in the new cathedral of Saragossa; and to St James of Compostela.

This, however, is not the whole of Spain. The heart of Spain and of the Spaniard is still heavy with the weight of many secrets, an astonishing mixture of passion, chivalry, heroism and inconsequence—a very Gordian knot of mystery, impossible to disentangle. Something of the atmosphere of this mystery is conveyed to the non-Spaniard in *La Vida nueva de Pedrito de Andía*, a novel by Rafael Sánchez Mazas. This offers more than bull-fights and folklore—a picture of the bourgeois society of Bilbao and the Basque country, and especially, the story of the youthful affection of Pedrito and Isabel. At fourteen the boy Pedrito is growing up more slowly than Isabel, whom he has always regarded as his fiancée, and his love for her seems to be in jeopardy; but love triumphs, and the young couple meet again one on either side of the wall between the gardens of their family houses, by the door once so often opened, to exchange once more the passwords of earlier meetings—this time a prelude to their betrothal: 'If it's you, if it's me, I shall open.'

If all those who truly wish to know and understand the men and cities of Spain will knock thus upon her door, Spain will surely open to them.

The rôle of the picadors consists in tiring and maddening the bull at the beginning of the bull-fight without inflicting any deep wound, and this is accomplished by pricking the animal with a lance from the vantage point of the saddle.

Ready for the fray, these three men are smoking and chatting while they wait for the procession which initiates the fight. Their dress is not as magnificent as the glittering regalia of the matador, to whom falls the honour of the kill; it comprises, as described by Théophile Gautier, 'a short, open jacket, of orange, crimson, green or blue velvet, heavily embroidered in gold and silver, with sequins, passequilles, fringes, buttons worked in filigree and various similar embellishments, principally on the epaulettes where the original material has disappeared altogether under a glittering and luminous accumulation of interlacing arabesques; a waistcoat in the same style; a ruffed shirt, a loosely-knotted tie, a silken belt and tawny buffalo-hide trousers padded and lined with cloth, like a postilion's boots, in order to protect their legs against blows from the bull's horns; a grey hat or *sombrero*, with wide brim and shallow crown.' The weapon of the picador, adds the writer, 'is a lance surmounted by a point an inch or two in length.'

62
THREE PICADORS
IN THE SEVILLE
BULL-RING

The picadors are waiting . . . Meanwhile the posters announce a series of remarkable fights, which we should do well to attend. To neglect the opportunity to see at least one bull-fight is to neglect a basic aspect of Spanish life. They are easy to follow and identical throughout the country. Proceedings open with the procession of the toreros, headed by the *alguazils*. Next come the matadors themselves, followed by their *cuadrilla*: the *banderilleros* and the *picadores*. Ring attendants and mule team bring up the rear. The brilliant costumes, peculiar hats, the excellently co-ordinated tableau of this procession confer momentarily upon the plaza an archaic and romantic air.

63
BULL-FIGHT
POSTER IN
SEVILLE

This impression is, however, rapidly dispelled. Suddenly unleashed into the bright light of the arena, the bull rushes headlong in.

In the early stage of the fight a certain number of episodes take place in a strictly pre-established order. First the picadors must spear the bull with their lances, after which it is the turn of the banderilleros with their banderillos, which, stuck into the bull's hide and striking against its flanks, weaken it by loss of blood, at the same time driving it to fury. Next comes the *faena*: a series of passes executed by the matador, who plays the bull with his *muleta*, a piece of red material attached to a wooden stick.

When the animal is sufficiently enfeebled and excited, the matador proceeds to the kill, which may be either swift or prolonged. If the thrust is well-executed, the sword correctly plunged between the shoulder blades, the bull collapses on the spot. A mule team, accoutred with varying degrees of extravagance, drags away the corpse while the toreros parade around the ring acknowledging the acclamations earned by their bravery or their skill.

64
CAPITAL IN THE
CLOISTER OF
THE CHURCH AT
ESTANY

Beside the medieval church of Estany, on a Catalonian by-road not far from Vich and Manresa, stands a romanesque cloister decorated with singularly engaging carvings. The bucolic scene here is far removed from the cruelty of the bull-ring; on the capital of this particular pillar a bull is playing on the viol!

65
SALUTE TO THE
MATADOR

The last fights were splendid. After the kill, the toreros received the acclamations of the crowd. Perhaps today's fights will be even better . . .

66
THE PASS OF THE
MULETA

Banderillos have already found their mark. As the bull rushes forward, the matador makes his pass followed by a *volte*, and the animal which had been coming at him headlong draws up sharply, astonished to encounter only empty space instead of the red rag at which he had been rushing.

67
THE PLAZA DE
TOROS AT
PAMPLONA

The spectacle offered by the crowded tiers of the bull-ring—whether in Madrid, Barcelona, Seville, Valencia, or in less important cities such as Pamplona—is always astonishingly vivid and colourful. The Plaza is divided into two: the tiers of seats on the expensive, or shady side, and those exposed to the full glare of the sun, which are naturally sold more cheaply. Amid the flutter of innumerable cloth or paper fans, the crowd respond with their cries to the passes of the matador. The *aficionados*, or devotees of the ring, wax indignant whenever the toreros seem to them to be failing in courage or skill.

For a description of the emotions experienced by one present we turn once more to Gautier: 'When I emerged from the aisle to take my seat,' he recounts in his descriptions of his visit to Madrid, 'a kind of dazzled giddiness came over me. Cascades of light flooded the arena . . . Above the arena floats, like some evening cloud of mist, the clamour of the crowd. On the sunny side flicker and shine myriads of fans and tiny circular parasols fixed on stems of reed, like a many-coloured flock of birds preparing to take flight. Not a seat is empty. I assure you that it is in itself an admirable sight to see twelve thousand spectators gathered in so vast a theatre, where only the brush of God himself, dipped in the palette of eternity, could paint a ceiling in so glorious a blue.'

In order to dominate the bull from a better vantage point, the picador is perched on a high saddle. The belly of the horse is protected by a covering, sometimes made of wicker, against which the horns of the bull flounder. The picador then presses his lance with all his weight against the animal's back. Between the tiers of seats and the ring itself is a corridor protected by wooden boards (*tablas*) serving to isolate the spectators. Into this corridor, where stand a few privileged *aficionados*, the toreros are allowed to leap when pressed too closely by the bull.

68
THE TASK OF THE
PICADOR
(Barcelona bull-ring)

On the balustrade of the upper flight of the staircase in the University of Salamanca a horseman is shown attacking a bull: encounters of this kind once formed part of the festivities observed on the occasion of the granting of University Doctorates. The scene is made more picturesque by the charm of a surround dating from the earliest days of the Renaissance, of floral designs and scrolls, making a lace-like tracery.

69
SALAMANCA:
THE UNIVERSITY
STAIRCASE

The banderillero, after inciting the bull to charge, goes out to meet him, jumps aside and plants the banderillos in his hide. He then moves away while the bewildered beast registers the presence of something foreign in his body—the flapping sticks which cause a painful smarting in his back and flanks. (Plate 70; Cordova. Plate 71; Pamplona.)

70–71
THE TASK OF THE
BANDERILLERO

72
DESCABELLO
(in the Saragossa bull-ring)

The fight is almost over. The thrust has been delivered, but the bull, still on his feet, resists the kill. The matador, with the help of a special sword, deals the *coup de grâce*, which finishes off the animal by severing the spinal cord.

73
CLOISTER IN
THE CATHEDRAL
OF GERONA:
detail of a capital

In the very heart of Gerona, the cathedral and its cloister form a city within a city, pious and medieval in its atmosphere (Plate 134). One of the capitals of this cloister, like that of Estany (Plate 64), bears a charming and lively carving of a bull. On what strange spectacle can the gaze of the astonished animal be fixed?

74
AN EPISODE
OF THE KILL:
Barcelona bull-ring

Bristling with banderillos, the bull has succeeded in tearing the muleta from the hands of the matador, who, sword in hand, has been obliged to seek ignominious refuge in the direction of the *tablas*, while his assistants distract the attention of the bull, thus giving their master time to prepare for a fresh attack.

75
THE REMOVAL OF
THE DEAD BULL
(Saragossa bull-ring)

Now the bull is dead. The glorious fighting beast has met his end and is dragged from the arena by galloping mules bedecked with feathers. The setting sun allows a generous shade to fall upon these sad remains and on the vast arena with its patch of blood-stained sand.

76
HOLY WEEK IN
SEVILLE:
halt of the *costaleros* during a
procession

Here a parish or Brotherhood procession has come to a halt in the city streets. The incense-bearer wipes his forehead. The sturdy *costaleros*, or carriers, have emerged from beneath the float, under which, during the procession, they remain unseen and unseeing, guided by the floatmaster or *capataz*. Each float or *paso* is carried by a group of these *costaleros*, varying in number. The transverse bar of the float rests upon the back of their necks, which are protected by a wad of sacking wound around their heads and falling to their shoulders.

77, 78, 86–88
CARNIVAL:
dances and disguises at
Pamplona

Pamplona celebrates St Firmin from 6th to 12th July and La Chiquita from 25th to 30th September. The former is the better known festival, for it is then that the young bulls are unleashed in the city streets so that all comers may test their courage and their skill by playing the matador. At Carnival time the crowd invades the steep, narrow streets of the old town to admire the giant puppets on their triumphal procession.

For long Madrid extended no further than the immediate vicinity of the Moorish Alcázar; then it was transformed first into a Christian fortress and later into a royal palace, becoming, thanks to its status as the residence of Philip II, the seat of the Court and capital of the country; yet despite this, the town of Madrid did not even possess the right to call itself a city. The old quarters sloping down in the neighbourhood of the *Calle de Toledo* towards the Manzanares have retained something of their ancient atmosphere: picturesque, dirty, rather squalid. The *Plaza Mayor* of Juan Gómez de Mora is still the most remarkable architectural group; this is the former site of the famous *autos-da-fé* and of the great bull-fights. Towards the east, however, near the monastery of San Jerónimo and the Palace of Buen Retiro built by Philip IV, efforts at town planning undertaken by Charles II resulted in the creation of the *Paseo del Prado*. While the nineteenth century saw the spread of the residential quarter, the twentieth has seen Madrid gradually but unmistakably grow to resemble an American city. The *Calle de Alcalá*, several miles long and culminating in the *Puerta del Sol* (the actual gateway disappeared during the last century) runs almost the entire breadth of the centre of Madrid. Here we see the crossroads into which runs Madrid's magnificent modern thoroughfare, officially bearing the name of José Antonio Primo de Rivera, founder of the Falange, but commonly referred to as the '*Gran Vía*'. After a short rise, this thoroughfare runs in a graceful curve towards the *Plaza de España*. Flanked by high buildings, it boasts what was for long one of the chief curiosities of the city: the Telefonica 'skyscraper', visible in the background of the picture; however, this tall building has now been dwarfed into insignificance by those recently constructed on the Plaza de España, which have completely disrupted the scale of neighbouring architecture.

79
MADRID:
corner of the Calle de Alcalá
and the Gran Vía
(on the right)

Only in Spain can we still see such charmingly old-fashioned scenes as this and the one that follows. The young soldier strolls through the streets in company with a nursemaid in white collar and apron. She leads her employer's child by the hand, and has taken advantage of their daily walk to arrange to meet her suitor.

80
SARAGOSSA:
the soldier and the
nursemaid

These Andalusian ladies, severely but elegantly dressed in black, wear the traditional lace mantillas, beneath which are hidden their high tortoise-shell combs. Rosary in hand, they are doubtless on their way to church to attend a service in celebration of Holy Week.

81
SEVILLE:
Andalusian couples

82
BARCELONA:
general view of the city
from the Tibidabo

While Madrid is the political capital of Spain, in almost every other respect Barcelona is a more important city. During a long period in the Middle Ages it was the capital of an independent Dukedom. After it was united with the Kingdom of Aragon, Mediterranean trade contributed greatly to the prosperity of the port and to the enrichment of the town. Conquered and subsequently abandoned by the armies of Louis XIII, heavily punished by Philip V for heroically supporting the cause of his rival, the Archduke Charles, Barcelona made several valiant recoveries. It is now the centre of the most economically powerful region of Spain, and is a true metropolis as well as one of the great ports of the Mediterranean. In the course of the nineteenth and twentieth centuries the town has constantly given expression to the impatience of the Catalans—proud of their history, their language, their civilization, and fully conscious of their strength—in face of the political authority of Castile and Madrid. Their aspirations to a more important rôle within the state, or a larger measure of autonomy, have been for several centuries a major feature of Spanish history.

The medieval city, long clear of ramparts, contains a number of remarkable monuments: the cathedral, the *Audiencia*, the *Palacio Real Mayor*, the *Plaza del Rey* are all worthy of study. Philip V ordered the destruction of a whole district in order to build a citadel which would dominate the entire city. The Montjuich park contains the principal museums: the Archaeological Museum and the Museum of Catalan Art as well as the *Pueblo Español*, built for the 1929 Exhibition and reproducing typical streets and squares of the various regions or Provinces of Spain. On the other side of the famous *Plaza de Cataluña* stretches the geometrical extension of the city, the *ensanche*, where the roads all meet at right angles, cut by a single oblique thoroughfare called *La Diagonal*.

The city is dominated by a number of hills; there are those bordering the Citadel and Montjuich parks along the seafront; *San Gervasio*; *La Montaña pelada* and *Santa Eulalia* further inland. A funicular leads to the summit of the Tibidabo, over 1,500 feet high, on which stand a modern church dedicated to the Sacred Heart, an observatory and a fun fair, and which commands a view over the entire city: the *ensanche*, the old city, and the port with sea beyond.

83
DANCERS DURING
THE *Feria* IN
SEVILLE

The liveliness of Seville in Holy Week has made of it a great popular occasion. The *Feria*, on the other hand, has never been anything but profane. It takes place from 18th to 21st April on the *Prado de San Sebastián*. All the great local families open small booths or *casetas* in which they receive their friends and organize entertainment in their honour. Couples on horseback add a note of elegance. The *Feria* is an outburst of high spirits and gaiety—aristocratic as well as popular—full of fun and poetry.

We have already spoken of the 'double image' of Spain. There is the Spain symbolized by Victor Hugo's Infanta in 'La Rose de l'Infante':

> *A tiny figure, in the care of her duenna,*
> *In her hands she holds a rose, and watches.*
> *Watches what? She knows not. Water;*
> *A pool shaded by pine and birch,*
> *Before her a white-winged swan,*
> *And rocking waves beneath the singing branches,*
> *Secret depths of radiant, flower-filled garden.*
> *A beautiful angel, moulded out of snow.*

This is the Spain of austerity, of poetic sadness, and of the melancholy already possessing the life and soul of so young a Princess, a Spain soon to be tragically stricken by the destruction of its Invincible Armada. But these dolls in the shop-window of a street in Barcelona evoke the other face of Spain—Spain eager for life, the Spain of gay traditions, a dancing Spain whose women love to inflame the hearts of men.

Within a bend of the Tagus and set upon the slopes of a craggy spur of land, Toledo is like a vessel weighed down by the ages, stranded between the deep-sunk river and the torpid sun. We should obtain our first view of this vessel at some little distance from the opposite bank; only then should we enter the city, as though boarding it, by the bridge of Alcántara or of San Martín. And it is best to walk at random—leaving chance and time to reveal both the architecture and character of the city.

The *Ermita del Cristo de la Luz* is a former mosque (980), the main evidence of Moorish domination. *Mudéjar* art is represented by *Santa María la Blanca*, the *Tránsito* and the *Casa de Mesa*. The Catholic sovereigns commissioned Juan de Egos to build the monastery of *San Juan de los Reyes*. Charles V began the construction of the Alcázar, in which General Moscardo organized a brave resistance at the outset of the Civil War. It was long left in a half-ruined state, in an understandable spirit of pious remembrance, but its buildings are now in course of restoration.

The *Casa del Greco* is a poetic reconstruction of a sixteenth-century Toledo mansion containing a fine collection of paintings. The house is filled with memories of the great artist to whom it is dedicated. Was it not in Toledo that El Greco found the ideal setting for his ardent genius? The spiritual life which finds expression in his work is closely akin to the secret fire which seems to consume the great ship of Toledo when the evening sun fills the streets, setting aflame the roof of the most magnificent of all its monuments, the great gothic cathedral.

90-93
GLIMPSES OF
EVERYDAY LIFE:
quiet backwaters in sun
and shadow
90 *Limpiabotas* (shoe-shine
boys) at Jeréz de la Frontera; 91 Embroideress at
Ronda; 92 Clothes-mender
at Ronda; 93 A shady corner
of the old town of Gerona

These scenes of humble, everyday life, gathered at random in little Andalusian towns like Ronda or Jeréz de la Frontera, or in Catalan cities like Gerona, are full of a peaceful poetry. Surely there are too many *limpiabotas* in proportion to the population? But in this region all work is difficult to find, and in spite of his efforts no one client can offer more than a single pair of shoes to shine. Moreover the alternating touch of sun and shade soon reconciles the true Andalusian to intermittent activity. The embroideress and clothes-mender of Ronda alike exemplify the continuity in Spain of domestic activities or crafts which in so many other countries have been pushed aside by the pace of modern life. If he so desires, the modern traveller may bring back from Spain not only lace specially fabricated for the tourist but bed or table linen embroidered by patient Spanish hands.

94-97
CATHEDRAL OF
ST JAMES OF
COMPOSTELA:
Portico de la Gloria

Not only is St James of Compostela of major importance to Spanish Catholicism, but the town and its cathedral are intimately bound up with the whole spirit of medieval Christendom.

According to tradition St James the Greater was martyred in Judea on his return from the evangelization of Spain. His body was brought back to Spain after a miraculous journey across the sea, disembarked at Iria Flavia (that is, at El Padron in Galicia), and buried a short distance inland. The exact place of burial was lost to memory during the persecutions, but in the course of the great struggle between Christian Spain and Islam, the cult of St James, the patron saint of Spain, gained considerable strength. A distortion or misinterpretation of a passage in the text of the Apostolic Catalogues led to the belief that the Apostle had been buried in a marble tomb, and, in approximately the year 800, the remains of the Saint were discovered on the spot where now stands the cathedral of Santiago, in a 'marble tomb' which then formed part of the cemetery (*compostela*) of a former Roman township. The cult of the Saint, at first only local, was bound up with the defence of Christian Spain and the Reconquest, eventually becoming the most important in the whole of medieval Western Christendom. A great network of well-known routes converged on Santiago. Pilgrims from France passed through Toulouse and Somport, or set out from Le Puy, Vézelay or Tours and made their way into the peninsula by way of Ronceveaux. The various roads converged into a single track at Puente-la-Reina.

Along the remaining part of the journey the principal stages were Logroño, Nájera, Burgos, Frómista, Sahagún, León, Astorga and Ponferrada. These pilgrim routes with their constant procession of the faithful, and the links between the French and Spanish clergy arising from this pilgrimage, have both been powerful factors in the penetration of French civilization south of the Pyrenees.

The cathedral of St James of Compostela, along with that of St Sernin of Toulouse, represents the perfected model of the shrine or church designed for the worship of relics, the organization of processions, the circulation of pilgrims—a model previously attempted in the churches of St Martin of Tours and St Martial of Limoges. Santiago cathedral, begun in 1078, was completed, as far as the main body of the church was concerned, round about the year 1125. It was then in the state described in a famous text, the *Guide of the Pilgrim of St James*. A little later, between 1168 and 1188, the main façade was embellished by the addition of the *Portico de la Gloria*, signed by the master-sculptor Mathieu. The baroque period, which left the interior untouched, almost completely surrounded the exterior with new buildings, very different in style but no less magnificent, so that the *Portico de la Gloria* now stands to the rear of the *Obradorio* of Fernando de Casas y Novoa (1738–1749). This porch may be compared to those tympanums which are the eternal glory of French medieval sculpture—at Vézelay, Autun, Moissac, Conques. Yet there is a touch of true originality in the treatment of relief and movement, which are much more emphatic and characteristically Spanish. The *Portico de la Gloria* comprises a great central portal with tympanum and mullion treating the theme of the Church of Christ, and two smaller lateral doorways without tympanums, the left-hand door being dedicated to the Church of the Jews and that on the right to the Church of the Gentiles.

On the tympanum of the main doorway is a Christ the Redeemer, between the Evangelists and Angels bearing the Instruments of the Passion; on the recessed orders are the Elders of the Apocalypse; on the pillars to left and right the Prophets of the Old Dispensation stand face to face with the Apostles.
The central sculptures thus take their place in a well-defined iconographical group: the capital represents the Trinity, while up the pillar climbs the Tree of Jesse. Above the capital, welcoming the pilgrims, stands St James the Greater, not visible in this picture. A touching and time-honoured custom requires that each believer should place his hand on the base of the Tree of Jesse; countless fingers laid upon this mullion throughout the centuries have worn the stone into a series of narrow grooves.

94, 95
CATHEDRAL OF
ST JAMES OF
COMPOSTELA:
Portico de la Gloria.
Central doorway, upper
and lower sections of
central mullion

This doorway is no doubt dedicated, in accordance with St Augustine's *De Civitate Dei*, to the divine call inviting the heathen to enter into the Kingdom of Christ. In the centre of the archivolts are small heads of God the Father and God the Son. The carvings on the right represent the vices of a life lived in ignorance of grace; those on the left show angels bearing children towards the House of God, their heads respectfully inclined towards the Creator.

96
CATHEDRAL OF
ST JAMES OF
COMPOSTELA:
Portico de la Gloria.
Archivolts of the right-
hand doorway

97
Portico de la Gloria.
Central doorway: the
Prophets of the Old
Dispensation

From left to right these prophets are Jeremiah, Daniel, Isaiah and Moses. Their names can be deciphered on the phylacteries or scrolls held out before them. The capitals above the first three prophets represent the capital sins, while above the head of Moses an angel holds a floating scroll on which appears a text concerning the Prophets of the Old Dispensation.

98
TARRAGONA
CATHEDRAL:
capital of central mullion,
cloister doorway: The
Epiphany

The aqueduct, the mantle wall and archaeological museum all remind us of the outstanding importance of Tarragona in the Spain of Roman times. After the Moslem invasion, and when the restoration of the Archbishopric had been made possible by the Reconquest, the construction of the cathedral served as an affirmation of the renaissance of the city and of its ecclesiastical rôle. Hence the beauty of the building, begun in 1171, and of the cloister added in the twelfth and thirteenth centuries; its decoration was entrusted to the workshops of the most important sculptors.

The same artist who carved the marble altar front of Santa Teclà was responsible for the capital of the mullion of the cloister doorway: here he represented, powerfully and movingly, the Birth of Christ, the visit of the Three Wise Men to Herod and the scene of the Epiphany. Declining to leave the smallest area uncovered, he multiplied the ornamentation and confined his scenes even more closely than was strictly necessary to fit them to the capital.

99
MONTSERRAT:
the Black Virgin

The eleventh century saw the foundation of a number of *ermitas* or hermitages in one of the most picturesque and majestic settings in the whole of Spain (Plate 13). Principal among them was Santa María, first mentioned in 888 and given to the monastery of Ripoll by Count Guiffre. In 1011 the authority over the hermitages of Oliva, the famous Abbot of Ripoll, was confirmed, so that for several hundred years (1074–1409) Santa María de Montserrat was no more than a priory in the Ripoll dependency. Enlarged over the years, it once more became independent, but was reduced to ruins during the Napoleonic wars. During the nineteenth century when the buildings were reconstructed, enlarged and decorated, it again achieved considerable prosperity and splendour.

The Black Virgin, patron saint of Catalonia, is worshipped in a *camarín* reached by a separate staircase of especial magnificence above and behind the High Altar. The Virgin is seated on a silver throne dating from 1947. Legend has it that the statue was sculpted by St Luke, brought to Spain by St Peter and discovered not far from the present monastery in the *Cueva de la Virgen* in the year 880. In fact it is difficult to fix the date of this work with any degree of accuracy, but it was probably executed between the late eleventh and the thirteenth century.

Contradictions of style are often only apparent to certain connoisseurs and scholars of over-exquisite sensibility. The cathedral of Gerona (see note on Plate 134) has something over and above the usual atmosphere surrounding great medieval monuments—an aura of age-old piety, intimate and withdrawn. Yet the cathedral with its three-tier baroque façade, standing at the summit of a monumental staircase, composes a particularly successful vista.

This scene would not be out of place among our earlier evocations of sun in the daily life of Spain. Yet it is more than a mere episode of life in Palma—the composition of the picture is interesting in itself. The gradation of shadow contrasts with the triumphant white of the wall; the depressed arch and the crucifix preserve the picture from over-rigidity, and the black-robed figure adds movement to the purely plastic qualities of the scene.

In 1946 the sculptor Federico Marès, to whom we owe the restoration of the statues of the Kings of Aragon on the tombs at Poblet, presented to the City of Barcelona several remarkable private collections of works of art. These included statues dating from the Middle Ages to the sixteenth century, examples of the art of gold- and silversmiths, fans and ceramics. These pieces were installed in the former *Palacio Real Mayor*, forming the Museum which bears the donor's name. This late romanesque *Virgin and Child* claims our attention by its intensity of feeling and almost savage vigour of form.

When the effigies of the Sorrowing Virgin are borne through the streets of Seville in Holy Week, from parish church or Brotherhood chapel towards the great cathedral, we may witness, besides the worshipping in the streets of the Sorrowing Mother of Christ, a public celebration of the triumph of a Goddess. The crowds of the faithful cross themselves or bow their heads in prayer: a few may even raise a cheer. The innumerable candles flaming before the statue are like a fiery bank of flowers. The flash of precious stones and gold embroidery lights up the Virgin's crown and train. There is an astonishing contrast between the tragic face of the statue, the overwhelming luxury of its jewels and costume, and the excitement of the crowd, at once devout and familiar.

106
A WINDMILL
NEAR
CARTAGENA

'Upon this there rose a little wind and the great sails of the mills began to turn, seeing which Don Quixote spoke as follows: "You may wave more arms than those of the Giant Briareus, but I shall make you pay for it." So saying he recommended himself with all his heart to his Lady Dulcinea, begging her to succour him in this hour of danger; then, well protected by his buckler and with his lance poised at the ready, he dashed forward on the galloping Rosinante to attack the first mill lying in his path, driving his lance into its sails. At this moment the wind made the sail revolve with such violence that the lance was shattered, carrying with it horse and horseman who were both sent rolling some way off into the plain.' (Cervantes, *The Ingenious Hidalgo Don Quixote de la Mancha*.)

The humanity and force of this episode are revealed by the fact that however often it is recounted it never becomes stale or hackneyed. Cervantes makes fun of the *hidalgo* raised on tales of Chivalry, yet at the same time admires and loves him, for Don Quixote personifies the noblest aspirations of the Spanish soul towards unselfish action.

Plates 62-106

64

65

63

66

68

69

70

71

73

74

72

80

81

83

82

84

85

86

89

87

88

90

95

96

94

98

99

100

101

102

The Christs of Spain

*I take and utilize the indivisible universe created by God at a
single stroke, and with which, under His holy will, having
renounced my own, I am intimately blended,*
*The past, which, with the future, forms one indecipherable
substance,*
The sea, placed at my disposal . . .

The Jesuit Father in *Le Soulier de Satin,* by
PAUL CLAUDEL

SPAIN has proved that she is as intimately linked with Christ, with his celestial love and
the representation of his earthly life, as Claudel's Jesuit was bound to his mast and
united to the ocean, which, heaving beneath the broken vessel, was preparing to swallow
up for all eternity both man and boat. Half-way between Europe and America he called
down upon the latter a heavenly benediction: 'May her blessing be that of Abel the
shepherd amid his rivers and his forests. May war and dissension be spared her. May
her shores never be sullied by Islam and the yet direr plague of heresy.' The Jesuit
might well have pronounced such words quite independently of his martyrdom upon
the mast, for, in spite of bloody strife and shameful incidents, it was to the Cross of
Christ that the New World was offered up by Spain.

But what need have we to seek in the heart of the Atlantic ocean a shipwrecked vessel
and an imaginary martyr? Spain herself offers a wealth of testimony to the Saviour: in
the spirit of both land and people, in their daily life, their ceremonial and, of course,
their art.

No doubt all parts of Spain do not express Christ with equal conviction. Andalusia
remains suffused with the seduction of the Arab East, both because of its history and its
architecture, and on account of its atmosphere, which is of an ardent gaiety deriving

from both mind and spirit. It is tempting to imagine that after Adam and Eve were expelled by the Angel from the earthly paradise, there remained one region of the earth in which the brightness of the sun was never dimmed: the region of Cordova, Seville, Granada, Cadiz and Malaga. There are certain provinces whose physical aspect alone may prevent their turning the heart of man towards the Saviour: the languorous Levant on the shores of the generous Mediterranean; proud and arrogant Catalonia; the Basque Provinces, still full of the poetry of a green and tender country-side, though touched by the hand of industry; even Galicia—despite the pilgrims of Compostela—Galicia lost among her dreaming mountains and her rugged coasts.

But who can fail to feel awareness of the spirit of God in Estremadura, with its vast, barren landscapes? At Guadalupe with its famous Virgin and its monastery? At Yuste, chosen by Charles V for his last retreat? And above all in Old and New Castile, where the landscape expresses far more than a mere mood, symbolizing the resignation of the poor in spirit, the passionate impetus or the aridity of the contemplative, the burning gaze of the apostle, the unexpected crystalline freshness of the voice of the recluse? Often the night outdoes the day in intensity of fervour: then there arises from the earth, refreshed at last, a wave of calm serenity, like some spiritual mist, while from the starry firmament there descends an almost perceptible cloud of quietude. In a silence so complete that, beyond it, one may hear in imagination the murmur of the galaxies, man, alone at last, may think on God and, peradventure, find him. Thus it is not surprising that Old Castile should be the native province of St Teresa of Avila and St John of the Cross. While the harshness of the landscape certainly contributed to the approach of these saints to God, certain mystic love poems, on the other hand, describe a green and tender nature. Listen to the Bride in the *Spiritual Hymn* of St John of the Cross in her search for the Bridegroom:

> *My Beloved is like the mountains,*
> *like lonely, wooded valleys,*
> *like unknown islands,*
> *like rivers with sounding waters,*
> *like murmuring of breezes filled with love.*

Spanish painters, with an art equal to the strength of their conviction, have expressed a like fervent ecstasy and mystic aspiration or, at least, a like intensity of faith and spiritual life. The first impression created by the paintings of El Greco is surely one of entry into a spiritual universe. Zurbarán has portrayed the monks of Andalusia and Estremadura with a technical mastery and a sense of truth seemingly never attained by any other artist in the same type of portrait. Beneath their rough habit can be divined the peasant still close to his native earth, but attitude of body, carriage of head, ardour of gaze reveal them to be already wholly possessed by Christ. Murillo, who is sometimes considered to typify a certain mediocrity of religious emotion, apt to relapse into insipidity and affectation, displays on the contrary not only an exquisite tenderness but often an unsuspected vigour.

The *Christ* of the Prado represents a justly famous triumph of Velásquez: the crucified figure still scored by the tragic suffering of the Passion—drooping head, pierced side and bleeding hands and feet—yet transfigured by the radiance emanating from the heavenly face and the stark lines of the body!

In this Christ we find an exceptional synthesis of two fundamental trends in Spanish religious feeling: the purely spiritual and the concern with physical suffering. It is only too easy to point out the contradiction involved. However, the psychological unity of a people or an individual is not affected by apparently contradictory forms of expression, which are in fact complementary. The Spaniard aspires to find Christ in a burst of passionate love, but, in order to arouse in his soul the vital stimulus, he must first conjure up the terrible truth of his mortal agony. He must see for himself the body racked by horror, suffering and death.

The *Santo Cristo* worshipped in Burgos cathedral is typical of pathos carried to an extreme bordering on the monstrous. In the description of this statue left by Théophile Gautier accuracy and astonishment are nicely blended: 'No longer made of stone or painted wood but of human skin (or so, at least, it is alleged), stuffed with infinite care and art. The hair is real hair, the eyes have real lashes, the crown has real thorns, not a single detail is neglected. Nothing could be more dismal or distressing than the sight of this tall, ghostly figure stretched upon the Cross, apparently alive yet deathly still. The rank-looking, swarthy skin is marked with long streaks of blood so admirably imitated that you would swear that it was actually flowing.'

But quite apart from such examples of excessive realism, there remains the vast and magnificent domain of Spanish polychrome sculpture. While the religious feeling expressed by this sculpture is as poignant as it is abiding, it also displays great artistic originality. The monumental reredos of the churches and cathedrals of Spain, the *pasos* carried in the Holy Week processions, various major groups and isolated statues executed by the sculptors of the sixteenth, seventeenth and eighteenth centuries endlessly recount the glory of God and the life of Christ, the Virgin and the Saints. Each reredos is in itself an open book, full of colourful and striking pictures, filling every niche and corner from floor to vaulted roof. The harmony between the beliefs inculcated by the Spanish Church, the soul of the Spanish people and the talent—indeed, the genius— of Spanish artists is here complete. Polychrome sculpture cannot be separated from the churches which it decorates, cleaving to their stones as flesh to bone. It is as though the True God, in his distant paradise, had confided to them the task of peopling his sanctuaries, thus rendering his image accessible to man.

To this same genre belong the *pasos* carried in Holy Week processions throughout the length and breadth of the peninsula, assuming particular importance in cities like Valladolid and Cuenca—or in certain regions, such as Andalusia. The floats which are borne through the streets, escorted by hooded penitents, priests and *guardias*, surrounded by myriads of candles, represent both Madonnas with tear-stained faces and diamond-studded trains, and scenes from the Passion. Is there any valid reason why we should be shocked to find that such processions sometimes take place in an atmosphere of popular rejoicing? Today the inevitably spectacular element is exploited for the benefit of tourists, but we should try to understand such manifestations in their true light: a whole city, tumultuous but certainly also sincere and passionate, has come together to reconstruct and re-live the Passion—its laughter sometimes rivalling its prayers, its tears mingled with songs, penitence hand in hand with pleasure. When Holy Week is over, the whole of Spain has re-lived the last days of the Saviour and his death upon the Cross.

Thus it seems fair to say that while Christ may not be Spanish, at least no other people has succeeded so well in conveying to man the infinite, tragic suffering of Christ Crucified.

The two most important influences in the decoration of romanesque churches in Catalonia are undoubtedly those of Byzantine art and of the miniaturists. In these lies the key to the iconography of both apse and dome. Painting has, however, replaced mosaic as being a less costly medium. Many of these paintings have been removed from their churches and set up in the *Museo de Arte de Cataluña*, where they form a unique collection. Among the most famous are those taken from the churches of San Clemente and Santa María of Taüll, dating from the first half of the twelfth century. Reminiscences of these earlier works, and a minute attention to detail probably attributable to imitation of the miniaturists characterize the *Christ Pantocrator* brought to the museum from Esterri de Cardos. This now forms part of the decoration of the reconstituted apse in the museum, situated between the Evangelists, above the Virgin and a gathering of Saints.

Wilfred the Hairy, founder of Ripoll, was also responsible for the restoration in the year 875 of a former Visigoth monastery, situated a few miles to the east, further up the River Ter. There he established a female community under the authority of his daughter Emma—which accounts for the name *San Juan de la Abadesas*. The name persisted despite the fact that the nuns were replaced first by monks and later by regular canons. The church, begun in 1150, was to follow the pattern of French churches, with ambulatory and radiating chapels, but the proportions were not maintained, so that the nave appears puny in relation to the choir.

San Juan de la Abadesas has an admirable and monumental *Descent from the Cross*, dating from 1250, and possessing a rare simplicity and strength. It combines hieratic romanesque vigour with the dawn of a more personal interpretation of individual figures, now more than mere elements in the general composition.

107
FIGURE OF
CHRIST FROM
ESTERRI DE
CARDOS
Museum of Catalan Art,
Barcelona

108
SAN JUAN DE LA
ABADESAS:
Descent from the Cross

109
AVILA:
view of the city from the
Cuatro postes

Leaving Avila by way of the bridge over the Adaja, we soon come to a kind of small shrine consisting of four pillars around a crucifix, known as the Oratory of the *Cuatro postes*. From this vantage point the city with its towers and ramparts can be seen in all its spaciousness and beauty, as if it were a spiritual fortress. The little shrine is doubtless a place of pilgrimage and meditation. It was at the *Cuatro postes* that Don Francisco de Cepeda stopped the flight of his niece Teresa and her brother Rodrigo, doomed to perish in the Indies. St Teresa has related how constant reading of the lives of the martyrs led her to believe that theirs was the swiftest and surest road to the joys of Heaven. She persuaded her brother to accompany her into Moorish hands, where, they hoped, they would both be put to death. The naive heroism of such an attempt makes this one of the most touching incidents in the life of the Saint.

110
VIEW OF
SEGOVIA FROM
THE CALVARY

So intimate and natural is the harmony between Castile and Christian austerity that a Calvary has been raised even on the outskirts of Segovia, a city characterized by smiles and gaiety. This particular Calvary on the road to Avila dates from 1675. Its tragic crosses set the Passion against the tender sky—the Passion celebrated gloriously inside the great cathedral of the city.

111
PAMPLONA
CATHEDRAL:
Reredos in the chapel of
Santa Cristina

In the gothic cathedral of Pamplona—celebrated site of the tombs of Charles II of Navarre and Eleanor of Castile, which were begun by Jannin Lhomme in 1416—there stands also a small side chapel dedicated to Santa Cristina, with a great reredos painted in Flemish style towards the end of the fifteenth century. Each panel is occupied by a biblical figure holding a scroll bearing an inscription. But the power of this reredos is due above all to the carved wooden figure of Christ upon the Cross, radiant with a divine serenity despite the pathos of the flowing blood.

112
CORDOVA:
The Christ of the *Plaza
de los Dolores*

Night has fallen on the little square flanked by the Capucin monastery and the *Hospital de los Dolores*, and four lighted lamps surround the figure of Christ Crucified. Gradually, as darkness deepens, the religious symbolism of this Crucifixion diminishes—vanishes even—before a growing poetic beauty. Whether by starlight or moonlight, or the light of the lanterns alone, this *Christ* ceases to recall the Passion, becoming an unearthly vision, belonging rather to the world of aesthetic enchantment.

As charitable associations the Brotherhoods of Seville date from the reconquest of the city; their origin as groups of penitents seems, however, to date from 1533, the year of the return from Jerusalem of Don Fadrique Henriques de Ribera. During Holy Week their members are grouped according to trade, locality or other common association for a solemn procession from their church or chapel all the way to the cathedral. The precise processional order is well established. At the head goes the Cross, followed first by banners corresponding to the *pasos* and the standard of the Brotherhood, and then by floats bearing the statues of the Virgin and of Christ, surrounded by the penitents dressed in flowing robes, cloaks and hoods. Their garments are generally black or white, but may on occasion be red or green. These ranks of anonymous men, each one bearing a great lighted candle and remaining patiently in file despite the countless halts, give the streets of Seville in Holy Week a truly unforgettable atmosphere.

113, 114
HOLY WEEK
PENITENTS IN
SEVILLE

This sumptuous *paso* represents—according to the rules and with a naive and scrupulous attention to detail—one of the episodes of the Passion: Christ brought before the High Priest or Pilate, with a Roman soldier standing guard behind him. The white-robed penitents have broken ranks and the canopy of the float has been thrown back to reveal the *costaleros* seated on the pavement taking a brief rest before resuming the procession.

115
HOLY WEEK
IN SEVILLE:
A *paso* halts

Among the almost infinite variety of the decoration of Toledo Cathedral, the gigantic reredos of the high altar, executed in carved wood and painted in both gold and colour, is outstanding. It was executed for the most part in 1502 and finished, according to a commemorative inscription, as early as 1504, the year Isabella of Castile died; it represents the work of many different artists. Among the sculptors must be mentioned Diego Copin, Christian of Holland and Felipe Vigarny, and, among the painters, Jean of Burgundy. The various panels, surmounted by richly carved canopies, are dedicated to scenes from the life of Christ and of the Virgin, and the whole work is dominated by a Calvary.

These innumerable scenes, both artless and skilful in execution, suggest a comparison, if not an exact parallel, in the world of literature: for are they not the sculptural equivalent of a Mystery play such as Arnould Gréban's *Mystère de la Passion*? One of those magnificent, never-ending 'Mysteries' providing the men of the Middle Ages with an opportunity to narrate in a single setting the whole history of man, from the Fall to the Redemption through Christ's Passion.

116
TOLEDO
CATHEDRAL:
upper portion of the high
altar reredos

117
MURCIA:
Ermita de Jesús.
The Last Supper,
Francisco Salzillo

Born in Murcia in 1707, Francisco Salzillo was the son of a sculptor of Neapolitan origin established in that city. His first teacher was his father, and on the latter's death he was obliged to take over the direction of the family studio, renouncing his original intention to enter the priesthood. His life was spent almost entirely in Murcia, where he died in 1783. Salzillo is one of the last and most illustrious Spanish polychrome sculptors. His talent is far greater than the casual observer, seeing sentimental, insipid naiveté in his work, may believe. From his father's training, and the permanent links between Mediterranean Spain and Italy, came a bond with Neapolitan art, an art which has always found it easy—particularly in the Nativities for which it is especially renowned—to reconcile preciosity and popular emotion. From the religious vocation he had been forced to abandon Salzillo retained a fervent faith, enhanced by a vibrant sensibility. The peculiarly Spanish character of his art is evident in the masterly way in which he expresses in the faces and bodies of his saints, angels, Christs and Virgins, both ecstasy and suffering. In the work of Salzillo tenderness of heart and refinement of expression are combined in an atmosphere of suffering which is deliberate.

The major part of his work is to be found in Murcia and its immediate neighbourhood. The *Museo des Belas Artes* contains a Nativity crowded with figures. In the *Ermita de Jesús,* now a museum devoted to the art of Salzillo, are grouped many of his greatest works, notably his *pasos.* Here we may admire his *Christ in the Garden of Olives* and this *Last Supper,* which is both a realistic reconstruction of the scene and an outpouring of tragic religious emotion.

118
EL GRECO:
Christ carrying the Cross,
Prado

El Greco, the painter of Cretan origin whose name has become synonymous with Spain and with Toledo in the time of Philip II (see note on Plate 152) has left several representations of *Christ carrying the Cross.* Opinions vary as to the date to be attributed to that hanging in the Prado, painted not much later than 1591. But far more important than the date is the highly personal manner in which the artist has treated this theme. His Christ is beyond all physical and moral suffering: the crown of thorns has scarcely torn his brow, the cross does not appear to weigh heavily upon his shoulders, nothing about the translucent hands suggests the nails which are about to pierce them. The holy face is entirely absorbed in radiant contemplation.

119
BENAVENTE:
Church of San Andrés.
Christ by Estebán Jordán

It is impossible not to be struck by the contrast between the masterly serenity of El Greco's *Christ* and the tragic realism of this crucified figure, executed by one of his contemporaries, the Valladolid sculptor Estebán Jordán (*c.* 1530–1598). The right arm elongated by the weight of the body, the emaciated ribs, the bleeding face, the long drooping hair, everything is calculated to reproduce the full and almost unbearable horror of the reality of the Crucifixion. It will be observed that this horrific spectacle is presented against a setting particularly rich in carved brackets and gilt consoles, capitals, scrolls and foliage. The Spanish heart not only delights in exact renderings of physical suffering, but seeks to enhance such renderings by the contrast of a sumptuous setting.

Zurbarán, though he was born in Fuente de Cantos, Province of Badajoz, in the year 1598, and died in Madrid in 1664, spent most of his life in Estremadura and Andalusia, devoting himself specially to paintings commissioned by various local monasteries. The two most famous series are perhaps that of Guadelupe (1638–1639) which has remained within the monastery, and that of the Carthusian monastery of Jeréz de la Frontera (1633–1639), broken up in the course of the nineteenth century and divided between the museums of Grenoble and Cadiz. The portrait of the Carthusian Nicolo Albergati (1375–1443), an Italian cardinal who presided at the Council of Basel, hangs in the Cadiz museum. Zurbarán's art has a certain primitive quality sometimes bordering on clumsiness—probably the influence of his native province. Yet it possesses an element of Andalusian charm, particularly evident in his portraits of saints and angels, and is the expression of an ardent religious faith. He is *par excellence* a painter of monastic and religious life.

120
FRANCISCO
ZURBARÁN:
*The Carthusian Cardinal
Nicolo Albergati*, in the
Museo des Belas Artes,
Cadiz

A particularly tenacious legend long linked this picture with King Philip IV; but in point of fact this *Christ*, fastened to the cross by four nails in conformity with the iconographical rule observed in Seville during the first part of the seventeenth century, is based on a picture by the artist's father-in-law, the painter Pacheco. The history of this *Christ*, the most justly famous, perhaps, in the whole of eighteenth-century Spanish art, is long and chequered. The picture was painted in about 1632 and placed in the monastery of San Plácido in Madrid. Later it was the property of the Countess of Chinchón, forsaken wife of Manuel Godoy. This lady consented to sell it to the Prado, but her death intervened. Finally the picture came into the possession of Ferdinand VII who presented it to the Prado in 1829.

121
VELÁSQUEZ:
Christ upon the Cross, Prado

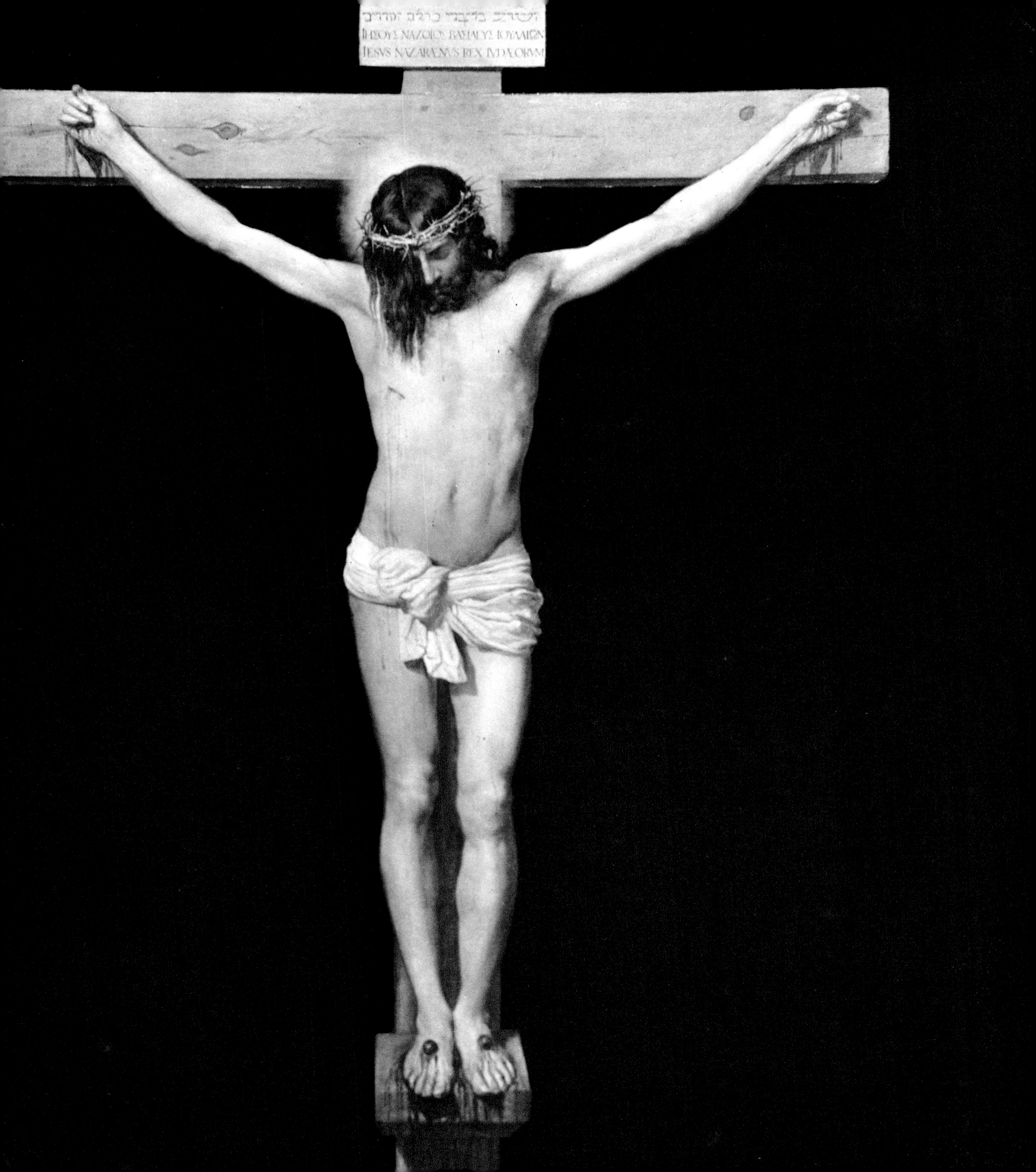
IESVS NAZARAENVS REX IVDAEORVM

123

Spanish Time

Spain, Spain, Spain,
Two thousand years of history have not sufficed to make you,
How can one not love, sadly, your lost past,
Love with hate and anger the lost present!

EUGENIO DE NORA

THE HEARTS OF NATIONS beat to a dual rhythm: one beat is that of nature, of changing seasons, sun and darkness; the other that of history, also marked by dawns of promise, brilliant noons and melancholy sunsets.

Spain has known many variants of this double rhythm. In its heyday it appeared as if the Creator had suspended in its favour his established time, causing all men to observe the time of Madrid, Toledo or Seville. In periods of misery and affliction, when the years appeared as endless as the misfortunes they accumulated, it was, on the contrary, as though time alone moved on again, leaving aside a Spain which the Creator had abandoned.

In the distant days of Roman domination, the beat of this dual rhythm seemed effortless. The majestic course of the sun and steady rhythm of the seasons was matched by the gravity and grandeur of the monuments raised in Roman Spain, seeming to show that the progress of the world and that of Rome marched at the same sure and steady pace. Have they not, indeed, continued to civilize successive generations for close on twenty centuries? But discord of nature and of politics crept in insidiously with the onset of the slow dissolution of the Empire. Spain in Barbarian hands yielded the astonishing and brilliant civilization of the Visigoth kingdom of Toledo, but after the landing of Tarik the Berber at Gibraltar, the tide of Moslem invasion surged up towards and across the Pyrenees, to be turned back only at Poitiers.

It was to take eight Christian centuries to undo a few years of Infidel time. While the Reconquest began almost at once with the victory of Covadonga in the Asturias in 718, it was to be completed only in 1492 with the recapture of Granada by the Catholic sovereigns. The long, terrible centuries between these dates can be regarded with the eye of the historian or the heart of the poet as a combination of strange, confusing rhythms. While the sky remained faithful to the immutable laws inscribed in Genesis, the Christians of Spain were peopling it with their faith: seeing in it a blessed firmament in which the souls of the chosen travelled on star-strewn paths preceded by the staffs of the Saints of God. The sky itself, so they believed, was on their side, even allowing the Knight Santiago, Bane of the Moor, to ride across it as though it were a common field of clover. To the casual view these eight centuries appear as the slow tide of the Reconquest unfurling southwards from the north. But this tide also had its advance and retreat: Moslem attacks once more threw into mortal danger a Christian Spain finally saved and brought to victory with the aid of the Popes, the Monks of Cluny and all the Chivalry of France and Europe. Yet how often was Spain racked by the internal dissensions of her own princes. To the rhythm of the Reconquest was added another rhythm, that of unification, achieved, if not territorially, at least in their persons, by Ferdinand of Aragon and Isabella of Castile. Hence medieval Spain was studded with both castles and Alcázars or Moorish fortresses. Hence, too, the epic of *The Cid*, a curious blend of guile and heroism, and the many deep cross-currents racing beneath the surface of medieval Spain.

Nor did the completion of the Reconquest, in 1492, unite the country in a single rhythm. Thanks to the discovery of America by Columbus, Spain began that very year to model upon its own heart that of a New World: the almost infinite lands and islands brought by the *Conquistadores* beneath the sceptre of its kings. Charles V, King and Emperor, heir to both Spanish and Habsburg lands, seemed for a moment to abolish time, and to annex a sun which never ceased to shine on one or other of his kingdoms. But Charles himself found this world rhythm beyond the compass of a single prince and, perhaps blinded by the brilliance of so much subservient sun, divided up his kingdoms, leaving to his son Philip II Spain, Flanders, Italy and the Indies. The flow of gold and treasure across the Atlantic into Spain began and grew apace. But these riches were used not to bring about a new economic order, but, all too frequently, to pay for costly wars, and also, more happily, for the creation of beauty. More than any other city it was Seville, home port of West Indian vessels, which profited by the discovery of the New World. The heart of this city beat to the rhythm of the capital of a great land-sea Empire. The swarming humanity in its streets and taverns and its colourful underworld have been described by Cervantes in one of his *Novelas exemplares*, entitled *Rinconete y Cortadillo*. The two boys of the title had no sooner arrived in Seville than they 'set out to visit the city and admire the size and splendour of its cathedral and the crowds along the river front. For it was the time of the provisionment of the fleet, and there they saw six galleys, which caused them to sigh and fear the day when their misdeeds should lead them to spend on the rowing benches the rest of their existence.'

Even after the division of the Empire of Charles V, the heart-beat of the Spanish kingdoms long remained that of the greatest power in all the world. But its sovereigns unwisely persisted in their grandiose and abortive schemes for European domination, laying themselves open to the charge of squandering the wealth of the Indies and of failing to appreciate the patience of the sun, its beams still fixed upon their lands.

For a time, under its own momentum, glory continued to lend these lands the light of its presence, but already, unobserved, the sun had resumed its independent course. That Spain was once more out of step with history was obvious at Rocroi, with the triumph of the Duke of Enghien, Prince of France and a great soldier at the age of twenty. Bossuet has described the fall of Spain in the face of the rise of France. 'At the very centre stood alone the mighty infantry of Spain, its close battalions like so many towers always able to repair their breaches, unshaken in the midst of all the rest in flight, launching their fire upon every side.' The splendour of Spanish art and literature outlived military and national glory, but soon it too sank into apparently hopeless decadence. It seemed that an eternal twilight was falling upon the Spain of Charles II, and that it was destitute of hope.

Then came the faint and modest dawn of Bourbon Spain. The new kings endeavoured to restore youth and vigour to the old nation brought beneath their sceptre by the will of the last Habsburg sovereign and the heroic ardour of Castile. But renaissance is never attained without struggle and the heart of Spain could scarcely find strength for the tasks of each hour. Yet, slowly, effectively, kings and ministers set Spain once more upon its feet, showing a skill and a persistence as wise and prudent as that of nature. Their work—a Frenchman must admit with shame—was undone by the armies of Napoleon and the upheavals which followed upon their Peninsular adventure.

The civil and religious wars of the nineteenth century and that of 1936–1939 have all too frequently stirred up the heart of Spain to a cruel and racing rhythm. This, in a world so far ahead of the Peninsula in so many fields, can only seem an extra mockery of fate.

Thus Spain, abandoned for two centuries on the shores of great nations, has been intermittently caught up by sudden sanguinary squalls, only to be thrown back again at once. The beat of its great heart has learned painfully to merge with the unchanging rhythm of Creation.

The aqueduct was probably built in the time of the Emperor Augustus to bring to Segovia the waters of the Acebeda which rises at the Puerto de la Fuentefría; its two storeys rise majestically on the eastern side of the city, and it gives its name to the square (*Plaza del Azoquejo*) which lies spread before it. The monument is even larger in reality than it appears in the picture, and surpasses in beauty those of Mérida and Tarragona. Composed of some one hundred and sixty arches, it extends for approximately 800 yards; at its beginning further east it barely rises above the level of the earth, and it mounts gradually as it proceeds. After a sudden bend, and having now attained two storeys, it branches north and, on the square itself, attains a height of nearly 90 feet. Continuing underground, it formerly carried water as far as the Alcázar, on the very edge of the rocky spur on which the city stands. Restoration took place between 1484 and 1489.

Between Segovia, city of joy and music, and the aqueduct, light despite its size and majesty, there is a subtle but undeniable harmony.

132
SEGOVIA:
Roman aqueduct from
the *Plaza del Azoquejo*

The little town of Egara, now Tarassa, was once the seat of a bishopric, created in the year 450 and swept away by the Arab conquest. The three churches of Santa María, San Pedro and San Miguel, separated from the modern town by the swift-flowing waters of the river and grouped together on a little hill, have caused many archaeological headaches and been the subject of both excavation and patient study. They are most probably Visigoth in origin, and there is also a suggestion that they were built at a time when the Moslem tide had receded from the region. Emphasis has been laid, too, on certain apparently romanesque features. The first two, Santa María and San Pedro, as they exist today, are composed of many elements, ranging from the paleo-Christian

133
CHURCH OF
SAN MIGUEL
DE TARASSA,
Province of Barcelona

era to the fourteenth century. San Miguel, which some historians date from the ninth century, has been tentatively identified as a baptistery, a hypothesis supported by the survival of the piscina. In fact, San Miguel, the most homogeneous of the three churches, is built on a square plan, with a minor apse on its eastern side. The as yet unsolved mystery of its origins and its reminder of remote times only serve to enhance, if possible, the lustre of its present radiant beauty.

| 134 CLOISTER OF THE CATHEDRAL OF GERONA | One of the most delightful novels recently published in Spain tells the story of a family in Gerona on the eve of the Civil War: *Los cipreses creen en Dios* (1953) by José María Gironella. The author admirably conveys the ecclesiastical atmosphere of the city— a climate which inspires the young Ignacio to enter the seminary, and, as a natural outcome, to gain a martyr's crown. |

The cathedral is the true heart and centre of the city. As it now stands, the edifice is gothic. The apse was begun in 1312, and work continued during the fourteenth, fifteenth and sixteenth centuries. Its main façade, which is baroque, stands superbly at the head of an enormous flight of steps (Plate 100). The cloister, however, is a vestige of the former romanesque cathedral. With that of San Cugat des Valles, it is the most remarkable in Eastern Catalonia. Some of its carvings, to which Arnal Castell probably contributed, are of purely ornamental motifs, such as stylized plants; others represent incidents from the Old and New Testaments in a charming style marked by its vividness, freedom and a keen sense of the picturesque.

The cloister of Gerona is of irregular shape, and has an atmosphere of poetic seclusion. Besides being the most perfectly typical example of romanesque architecture in Catalonia, it is a rare and privileged spot in the small provincial city, where the young and pure in heart may still hear God's call and devote themselves completely to his service.

| 135–139 RAMPARTS AND CASTLES OF MEDIEVAL SPAIN | Spain of the twelfth to the fifteenth century, with its opposing sallies of Moslem and Christian, conjures up in our minds cities sheltered by their walls, all-powerful castles in a vast, empty countryside. But we need not imagine these scenes from the past. Here in Spain they still rise before us, clad in age-old stones. |

| 135 THE RAMPARTS OF AVILA | The ramparts of Avila, the most complete and extensive in all Spain, are remarkable for the unity of their construction: they date principally from the twelfth century. On the eastern side, the apse of the cathedral is incorporated into the walls themselves. |

Their total length is a mile and a half, their average height 24 feet, and at intervals of 20 or 30 yards they are reinforced by towers.

From the base of the ramparts runs an arid stretch of country grazed by slow flocks of sheep. Lower on the slope stands St Teresa's Convent of the Incarnation. Beyond stretch the bare countryside and distant line of mountains. Over all, the pitiless Castilian light beats down through the pure air with extraordinary brilliance. It is rare indeed to find such complete identity between the site and architecture of a city, and its history and pervading spirit. The sky is both the sky of the medieval warriors and of St Teresa, the ramparts at once the bastion of the city and the entrance to a spiritual fortress.

The *Alcázar* dominates the confluence of the rivers Eresma and Clamores from a height of nearly 250 feet—a striking spectacle with its soaring spires, and so romantic that one might imagine that it sprang from the imagination of a nineteenth-century prince. It is curious that so ancient a fortress should suggest a comparison of this nature; dating from the Moslem occupation, it was enlarged and reconstructed by the Kings of Castile during the fifteenth and sixteenth centuries, and inhabited by their successors in the seventeenth century. The comparison is, however, not entirely without justification, for the Alcázar caught fire in 1862, and has since been restored. Today it is the home of the *Archivo general militar*. With the tower built by John II and the traces of *mudéjar* decoration it seems to come straight from the pages of some medieval history, yet it is tinged by its restoration with the romantic image of the Middle Ages forged by the nineteenth century.

136
SEGOVIA:
the *Alcázar*

In an Andalusia so deeply marked by Moslem domination, it comes as no surprise to find a church built shortly after 1264 on the site of a former mosque. It is fortified by four towers, one of which shelters the *capilla mayor*, and remains a remarkable building despite transformations effected between the fourteenth and sixteenth centuries.

Puerto de Santa María lies on the inner shore of Cadiz bay, into which the eighteenth-century galleons sailed home from the New World. In 1823, the 'Sons of St Louis', led by the Duke of Angoulême, came to deliver Ferdinand VII, then held prisoner by Cortès, permitting him to re-establish absolute power. Hence this fortified church conjures up mingled memories of Arab and Christian, of West Indian opulence and of nineteenth-century political convulsions.

137
PUERTO DE
SANTA MARÍA:
fortified church of the
Castle of San Marcos

138
CASTLE OF
GRAJAL DE
CAMPOS

Grajal de Campos, near Sahagún, is still a late-medieval and Renaissance city. The palace of the Dukes of Grajal was built in approximately 1540 on the model of that of the Alcalá de Henares. The castle, dating from the early sixteenth century, was specially constructed to allow the use of artillery. It was built in the form of a great square, with a tower at each corner, and detailed inspection reveals the care with which the gun emplacements and firing points were chosen. But the noise of fire-arms has long since died away, and beneath the ramparts, towering like a setting for some martial epic, is heard no sound but the song of birds and the cry of the farmer urging on his team.

139
CASTLE OF COCA,
Province of Segovia

Seen from a distance, the main body of this castle seems to disappear into a fold in the ground, so that when it stands revealed in all its power and complexity we are astonished at its vast size and its colouring—a fortress built of bricks burned by the centuries to a thousand different hues. Construction was authorized by John II of Castile on 15th July 1453, begun by that flamboyant prelate Don Alonso de Fonseca, and continued by his family. The castle is especially remarkable for its Tower of Tribute. Moslem influence is strongly marked, and the castle contains a number of interesting *mudéjar* paintings. Abandoned, the fortress long stood as a fantastic ruin, like some strange city aflame with sun and weighed down with silence. In 1954 it was presented to the nation by the Duke of Alba on condition that its restoration should be supervised by the Academy of San Fernando and the Ministry of Fine Arts. Work was completed in 1959, when part of the castle was assigned for use as an agricultural training school.

140, 142, 156
REMINDERS
OF THE
RECONQUEST

It is impossible to recall every incident, every detail of this major theme of medieval Spain. We must, however, here evoke the memory of the Cid, his life and tumultuous legend, and also pay our homage to the Catholic sovereigns who completed this medieval epic of the Christian faith with the recapture of Granada in 1492.

140
MONASTERY OF
SAN PEDRO
DE CARDEÑA:
the tomb of Rodrigo and
Ximena

Situated some six miles to the south-east of Burgos, the medieval monastery of San Pedro de Cardeña, despite its dilapidated condition, still contains the magnificent tomb of Rodrigo and Ximena, which forms a link with the Spain of the monks and warriors, the Spain of the Reconquest. According to the *Cantar de mio Cid*, written in approximately 1140, the hero, condemned to exile by Alfonso VI, King of Castile, was obliged to camp outside Burgos with his suite, since no one dared to give him hospitality. After borrowing money from the Jews—to whom he confided in exchange coffers containing not gold but sand, exacting from them a promise not to open them till a year had passed—the hero made his way by night to San Pedro de Cardeña to take leave of his wife and daughters, who had sought refuge in the monastery. The cocks were already bestirring themselves to crow, and the light of dawn already breaking through when the Cid arrived:

> *Apriessa cantan los gallos—e quieren crebar albores*
> *Cuando llego a San Pero el buen Campeador.*

Inside the church the monks were singing matins by the light of candles. Doña Ximena was at prayer. Monks, wife and children all hastened to the doorway, where the noble lady knelt before her husband, weeping and declaring that life, like death, already tore her husband from her. The hero spoke these words of comfort: 'Please God that I may live to see my daughters married and that times of happiness may lie ahead for all of you.' Summoned by the bells, the neighbouring inhabitants flocked round the Cid, kissing his hand and offering to serve him even at the risk of incurring royal anger. But the six days' respite allowed the hero had expired: the warrior and his suite departed to begin the ride which was to lead them to earn fresh laurels in the Moorish kingdom of Toledo, in Saragossa and Valencia. In the Abbey of San Pedro de Cardeña is preserved the tomb of El Cid and of Ximena, but their bodies lie in the cathedral of Burgos in the very heart of the *crucero*, illuminated by a radiance symbolic both of the terrestrial glory of the hero and of eternal light.

The Spaniard has always proved himself a skilful worker of copper, bronze and precious metals. Besides displaying style and technical proficiency, he has served the cause of art itself, and in decorating the door of a sanctuary, he is also bearing witness to his veneration of Christ and his Church. Thus, set among a series of political and martial scenes, the door-knocker of this plate plays a symbolic rôle, reminding us of the continuity of the genius of the Spaniard as creator of beauty and worshipper of Christ.

141
CATHEDRAL OF TOLEDO:
Door-knocker

The Catholic sovereigns originally decided that they should be buried in the Church of San Juan de los Reyes in Toledo. But in September 1504, after the recapture of Granada, they founded near the cathedral of that city the *Capilla real*, placed under the patronage of St John the Baptist and St John the Evangelist. The construction of this chapel was entrusted to Enrique de Egas, and it was completed in 1521. The chapel contains a number of famous works of art, including the sumptuous railing of Bartolomé de Jaén (*c.* 1520), the reredos of the high altar (Plates 143, 144) and, above all, the royal tombs.

142
GRANADA CATHEDRAL:
Capilla real. The tomb of Ferdinand and Isabella

The Florentine sculptor Fancelli was commissioned to construct that of Ferdinand and Isabella in 1512. The tomb was, however, probably actually executed between 1514 and 1517, after Isabella's death. The two sovereigns are portrayed at a fairly advanced age. The chapel also contains the tomb of Philip the Handsome and Mad Jeanne, their son-in-law and daughter, by Bartolomé Ordoñez, born in Burgos but trained in Italy (1519–1520).

143, 144
GRANADA
CATHEDRAL:
Capilla real. Details of the high altar reredos, showing the entry of the Catholic sovereigns into Granada and mass baptism of the infidels

Executed by Felipe Vigarny, 1520–1522, this reredos is still strikingly plateresque in style, particularly in the decoration of the pilasters and certain ornamental details. Its inspiration and technique are not difficult to define: a pungent realism, figured relief that is strong and colourful, and a broad and forceful composition. Dominated by a Calvary, this work is dedicated mainly to scenes from the life of Christ or to representations of St John the Baptist and St John the Evangelist, patrons of the chapel. It also displays, in the lower portion, episodes from the history of the reconquest of Granada by Ferdinand and Isabella. Thus one of the great triumphs of their reign and, indeed, of Spanish history, is commemorated within a few paces of their tomb.

145
BURGOS
CATHEDRAL:
The Constable's Chapel.
Detail of a pillar

After these reminders of the recapture of Granada, it is not inappropriate to recall those who followed the glorious enterprise of Ferdinand and Isabella in spirit. While the *Condestable de Castilo*, Don Pedro Hernández de Valasco, was fighting at Granada, his wife Doña Mencía Mendoza de la Vega obtained from Pope Innocent VIII and the Chapter of Burgos cathedral permission to have built, beside the apse, a chapel to house her own tomb and that of her absent husband. Every detail of the little chapel is enchanting: this pillar, besides its pictorial interest, is a reminder of men away at the wars and of the love of Christ, in whose name the battles of Ferdinand and Isabella were fought—shortly to be followed by those of the *Conquistadores* of America.

146
SEVILLE
CATHEDRAL:
Tomb of Christopher Columbus

In the background, on the left, can be seen a huge fresco representing St Christopher by M. Pérez de Alesio (sixteenth century), but our attention is naturally more strongly attracted by the tomb of Columbus himself. His body, which had been lying in Havana since 1796, was transported to Seville in 1899, after the emancipation of Cuba. It was then placed in a tomb executed by Arturo Melida in the cathedral transept, on the Epistle side. The heralds-at-arms of Castile, León, Aragon and Navarre bear the casket on their shoulders.

Columbus' son Ferdinand is also buried in Seville cathedral, near the main doorway. Ferdinand gave the Chapter both his own library and that of his father, which now form the 'Columbus Library' housed as an annexe to the cathedral on the *Patio de los Naranjos*.

147
SALAMANCA:
Façade of the University

Sculpted in the red-gold stone which lends such charm to the streets of Salamanca, smoothed by the centuries and softly gilded by the sun, the façade of the University of Salamanca (*c.* 1525) is a magnificent example of plateresque. (The term recalls the work of the old gold- and silversmiths, or *plateros*.) The work cost 30,000 ducats, and was conceived as a great stone reredos, applied to the wall of the building and extraneous to its architecture. On the lower tier, above the door, there is a portrait of Ferdinand and Isabella; on the middle tier appear the imperial arms, flanked by heads of Adam and of Eve, and above is the Pope upon his throne. The profusion of candelabra, foliage, tendrils and grotesques is exquisitely graceful. Yet the author of this masterpiece is unknown.

148
TRANSEPT
OF THE
CATHEDRAL OF
SIGÜENZA
Right: Jasper or Porphyry
door. Left: Doorway to
the Sacristry of the Santa
Librada Chapel

Between Madrid and Saragossa, in the centre of a calm green countryside, lies the little town of Sigüenza in the Province of Guadalajara. The patron of the city is Santa Librada, a young princess martyred in the kingdom of her father, King Catelio, during the Roman persecutions.

The cathedral, which was begun in the twelfth century, was considerably enriched and embellished during the sixteenth by a great bishop of Portuguese origin, Don Fadrique of Portugal, who died in 1539. Thus in the northern transept we find side by side several early sixteenth-century masterpieces: the reredos of the altar of Santa Librada (1515–1518), modelled on the tomb of Cardinal Mendoza in Toledo cathedral; the mausoleum of Don Fadrique, a few years later in date, and in which we see the hand of Alonso de Covarrubias; the Jasper or Porphyry door, so-called by virtue of the hard material employed on the older of its two surfaces, that facing the cloister (1507), and revealing, on its more recent transept side, a series of attractive plateresque motifs; and, finally, the door of the Sacristy of the Chapel of Santa Librada, with its elegant decoration in both plateresque and Renaissance style, contrasting oddly with the rigorous lines of the gothic gate itself, which is the work of Juan Francés and Martín García.

149–151
THE
MAGNIFICENCE
OF THE SPAIN OF
CHARLES V

Sovereign over many states in Europe and the Indies, soldier of the Catholic faith, Charles V spent little of his life in Spain. Nevertheless it was his Spanish kingdoms which furnished him generously with soldiers for his armies and which poured into his coffers the treasures of America. Both were necessary for the struggle with France or with the Protestants. Charles, prince of foreign origin, admirer of Italian and of Flemish art, introduced into Spain the beginnings of a Court art, sometimes very different in spirit from the art native to Spain.

149
MADRID:
Royal Palace, the
Armería

In the *Armería* stands the suit of armour worn by Charles V for single combat in the lists. Made by Colman of Augsburg (1526), it is embellished around the lower edge with hunting scenes, dogs in pursuit of stags and bears. The objects in the *Armería* form a collection unique of its kind, covering a period extending from the Middle Ages to the nineteenth century. The visitor who sees this collection for the first time cannot but be impressed by the splendid suits of armour, the effigies of princes and their horses, seeming to wait, transfixed in aimless joust, for the real combat to resume. The exhibits connected with Charles V himself are perhaps the most striking: there is, for instance, the suit of armour he wore on the day he beat the Protestants at Mühlberg, and the tent of Francis I of France at Pavia.

150, 151
THE ALHAMBRA,
GRANADA:
Palace of Charles V

There is a striking contrast between the halls and courtyards of the Alhambra—some intimate and mysterious, others large and majestic, but always juxtaposed without any particular plan, and built of bricks and mortar—and the Palace of Charles V, so monumental and regular, built of stone, and with the regard for geometry and harmony typical of the Italian Renaissance. Charles decided on the construction of the palace during the summer of 1526, spent with Queen Isabella at Granada. The architect was Pedro Machuca, a gentleman of Toledo, who had studied under Michelangelo in Italy and was well-informed not only on Italian architecture but also on all the artistic trends then current in that country. He returned to Spain about the year 1520, becoming Equerry to the Governor of the Alhambra, the Marquis of Mondéjar. Although famous primarily as a painter of reredos, Machuca gave unique and magnificent proof of his architectural knowledge in the palace of Charles V in the Alhambra. Work began in 1527 and continued after Machuca's death in 1550, partly under the direction of his son. The palace was completed during the seventeenth century. The roof, however, is a modern addition. The original plan, contemporary with the plateresque creations of Salamanca and Sigüenza, shows the extent to which art in Imperial circles had already evolved beyond that of the provinces. Pedro Machuca, reared on Vitruvius and Bramante, transposed into Spanish terms the inspiration, forms and ornamentation of the Italian Renaissance; his admirably harmonious circular courtyard was inspired by an architectural idea which his Italian predecessors had often praised but seldom realized.

History often confers on past periods a simplicity and unity they may never have possessed. Can we justifiably reduce the Spain of Philip II, as here, to a painting by El Greco and the Escorial, when the King himself refused to place the artist's *St Maurice* in the church of his new monastery? In both the work of the artist and the royal building religious considerations were vital, and this fact may serve to justify the simplification in the present instance.

152, 153
THE SPAIN OF
PHILIP II

El Greco was born at Candia, on the island of Crete, then under Venetian domination, in approximately 1541. He became a pupil of Titian in Rome, and seems to have appeared in Spain when aged about thirty-five. He is known to have been in Toledo in 1577, and it was in this city, whose name is now inseparable from his own, that his art attained its full originality. It was also in Toledo that he died in 1614. Not only was he the finest painter of Spanish society of his time but his power to represent the spiritual in life is unparalleled. He leads us into a world in which forms assume their true values only in relation to the spirit.

152
TOLEDO:
CHURCH OF
SANTO TOMÉ
The Burial of Count Orgaz,
El Greco

In the sixteenth century the rich and pious Don Gonzalo Ruiz de Toledo, Governor of Orgaz, rebuilt and endowed the church of Santo Tomé. He also encouraged the foundation in Toledo of a monastery of Augustinian monks within the parish of San Esteban. He died in 1323, and during his burial in Santo Tomé the assembled nobility and clergy of Toledo beheld St Augustine and St Stephen, descended from Heaven, take the body of the dead Count and lower it to the tomb with their own hands, declaring that such was the honour due to those who truly served God and his Saints.

This is the scene represented by the lower portion of El Greco's painting. The burial serves as an occasion for a magnificent gallery of portraits. The assembled company, possessed by absolute faith and incomparable serenity, does not appear at all astonished by the miracle. The upper portion, not here reproduced, is very different in inspiration and shows the soul of Count Orgaz arriving in Heaven, borne by an angel and received by Christ with the Virgin and St John the Baptist on either hand. The forms in this part of the picture are more ethereal. El Greco was commissioned to paint the *Burial of Count Orgaz* in 1586; the canvas itself bears the incorrect date 1579.

153
GENERAL VIEW
OF THE
ESCORIAL

Philip II founded and built the monastery of San Lorenzo del Escorial in gratitude for the victory won at St Quentin on 10th August 1557, anniversary of the feast of St Lawrence. The first stone was laid on 23rd April 1563, and the building was regarded as finished on 12th September 1584. Provision of fittings and the decoration of the interior continued, however, for several generations after this. The construction of the monastery, placed in the charge of the Hieronymites, was carried out first by the Italian-trained Juan Bautista de Toledo, who died in 1567, and subsequently by Juan de Herrera. Fray Antonio de Villacastín also made a vital contribution to the work, which was executed under the personal supervision of Philip II. Philip died at the Escorial in 1598. In the completion of this monastery, so much a part of the glory of Spain, Italian artists—painters and decorators particularly—played an important part; even under Charles II the painting of the vaulted ceilings of church, *coro* and great staircase was carried out by Luca Giordano.

The vast Escorial is a devout tribute—in stone, paint and precious metals—offered by the Princes of the House of Habsburg to the Christian God who, though he granted them victory and domination, is also the God of renunciation and death. The Escorial expresses some of the noblest qualities of the Spanish character: love of immensity combined with austerity—a Catholic vision of the universe.

The church is the heart of the Escorial. Inspired by St Peter's in Rome, it contains the monumental mausoleums of both Charles V and Philip II, executed by Leone and Pompeo Leoni. The Escorial is at once monastery, palace, museum and royal pantheon. The Chapter-houses contain many splendid paintings: El Greco's *St Maurice* and *The Dream of Philip II*, Ribera's *Jacob and the flocks of Laban*, as well as *Joseph's brethren* by Velásquez and many other pictures. Here, too, can be seen Titian's *Last Supper* and Rogier van der Weyden's *Crucifixion*. Claudio Coello's *Sagrada Forma* provides a series of fine portraits of Charles II and his entourage.

154, 155
VELÁSQUEZ
AND THE
COURT OF
PHILIP IV

Diego Velásquez, born in Seville in 1599, pupil and later son-in-law of the painter Pacheco, studied in the Sevillian school before settling in Madrid for life. Apart from two fruitful visits to Italy, he lived thereafter in the circle of King Philip IV, who honoured this artist with more than mere protection, a sympathy almost worthy of the name of friendship. The artist became, in fact, a kind of Grand Marshal of the Palace, and it may be that this office, and all that it represented in the way of social advancement, was more flattering to the soul of Velásquez than the renown he won by his work. It did, however, involve the artist in a series of practical tasks reaching their peak of intensity on the occasion of the King's journey to Fontarabie for the marriage of his daughter María-Teresa to Louis XIV. Velásquez died in Madrid at the age of sixty-one, shortly after his return across the Pyrenees. His pictures have bestowed the stamp of immortality upon Philip, his family and his Court, as well as upon himself. The work of Velásquez, always carefully elaborated, must be accounted one of the high points in the history of art by virtue of its technical perfection, its consummate freedom, and the genius with which the artist creates a life seemingly independent of himself.

154
VELÁSQUEZ:
Las Meninas, Prado

The picture shows us the artist's studio in the old Alcázar of Madrid (destroyed by fire in 1734 and replaced by the present *Palacio real*). Velásquez, standing before his easel, is painting the Infanta Margarita, to whom a Maid of Honour, kneeling on the left, hands a jug of water on a tray. Another Maid of Honour, a dwarf, and some attendants stand towards the right. In a doorway in the background can be seen Don José Nieto Velásquez, one of the palace functionaries. In the mirror near this door appear Philip IV and Queen Mariana.

The picture, which dates (1656) from the last years of the artist's life, combines perfect grouping with perfect naturalism. To combine so ingeniously painter and Infanta, to dispose her suite around her, and to herald the entrance of the King and Queen in a looking-glass must have required the utmost study, yet the plans of the old Alcázar show that Velásquez took no liberties with the actual disposition of his studio and, thanks to certain inventories, it has even proved possible to identify the pictures indicated on the walls. The difficult feat of grouping is accomplished by Velásquez in a scene of ordinary palace life.

Las Meninas is both a scene drawn from life and a creation of the hand and brain of Velásquez: it is artistic illusion attaining to reality.

155
VELÁSQUEZ:
Portrait of Philip IV, Prado

In this portrait, painted prior to 1628, Philip IV was not yet a sovereign weighed down by defeats, the melancholy old man of the last years of his reign, but a prince who still loved pleasures, fêtes, spectacles and dancing. Yet in this picture of a young man austerely dressed in black, we may perhaps catch a presentiment of the long series of disappointment which lay ahead. At least we can surmise the burden of a Court both frivolous and weighed down by etiquette, gallant and bigoted, rigid and divided, and, beyond all this, the paradox of a monarchy as weak as it was absolute.

There is a striking contrast between the simplicity of Velásquez as a portraitist and the pomp with which the painters of the House of Bourbon loved to surround their subjects. Velásquez was interested in the individual and, in this portrait, the dignity of the monarch derives from the man himself, whereas it is impossible to imagine the royal portraits of France, in which the desire for exact representation was predominant, stripped of the external trappings of monarchy.

156
THE ROYAL
PANTHEON
IN THE
ESCORIAL

The visitor who approaches the Pantheon of the Escorial with mind full of macabre literary allusions will find himself compelled to admiration and meditation of a different nature. The Pantheon is a magnificent baroque creation, greatly influenced by Italian art, in which the pomp due to royal majesty is preserved even in death. It was constructed beneath the church during the reigns of Philip III and Philip IV.

The plans for this funerary chapel were originally drawn up by Herrera, but were subsequently modified by the two architects Juan Gómez de Mora and Alonso Carbonell, as well as by the Italian decorator Crescenti (1617–1654). Beyond a bronze doorway bearing the date 1654, three flights of stairs lead down into the Pantheon, octagonal in design, embellished with pilasters, bronzes, and flanked on all sides by the royal tombs. The altar was designed by Carbonell, and the crucifix above it by D. Guidi; the altar front is by Fray Eugenio de la Cruz and Fray Juan de la Concepción. The chandelier is the work of the Genoese artist Virgilio Fanelli, while angels holding candelabra between the pilasters were carved by G. A. Ceroni.

In this Pantheon were laid to rest Spanish sovereigns from Charles V to Alfonso XII, Queens who were mothers of kings, and also Isabella of Bourbon, first wife of Philip IV. Philip V and Elizabeth Farnese were buried in the church of La Granja, and Ferdinand VI and Barbara of Braganza in the Salesas Reales in Madrid. Queens who were not mothers of kings, infantes and infantas were placed in rooms adjacent to the Pantheon, whose decoration dates from the nineteenth century.

157, 158
THE SPLENDOURS
OF BAROQUE
DECORATION

Decorative art, particularly that employing carved and gilded wood, attained astonishing splendour in the reredos and stalls of the seventeenth and eighteenth centuries. The rich appearance of the material, and with it the possibility of escape into a world of dreams, was intensified by the inventive faculties of architect and decorator. This is no anarchistic art, but one requiring particular skill and calling into play both sensibility and imagination, together with a love of spectacle, transporting the humble into a superhuman world in which their eyes are dazzled and their misery consoled by a magnificence which is a foretaste of Paradise itself. This art was so successfully practised —in Madrid and Salamanca during the reigns of Charles II and Philip V—by the Churriguera family, that the term 'Churrigueresque' has been derogatorily employed to describe it. Though the members of this family were the outstanding, they were not the exclusive exponents of this style. Mention must be made at least of Pedro de Ribera in Madrid, Narciso Tomé in Toledo, the Figueroa family in Seville, Hurtado in Granada and Fernando de Cases y Novoa in Santiago, to whom we owe the *Obradoiro*, the cathedral's famous baroque façade. And in point of fact, for more than two hundred years the whole of Spain worshipped God and his Saints, offered up their prayers and invocations to them, even imagined them having their existence, among the gold, the solomonic columns, the swirling pediments, the fretted panels of an infinite variety of seductive, capricious ornament.

The San José chapel in Seville is essentially the work of the guild of carpenters; it is, in fact, their private sanctuary. Both its architecture and its decoration have undergone a series of transformations. Two main stages of its history can be distinguished. The first, starting from the inception of the work, is from 1690 to 1717 and probably represents the execution of plans drawn up by Pedro Romero. The second period extends from 1747 to 1766. Stucco ornament, as well as carved and gilded woods, were employed in the decoration of this chapel.

The *capilla mayor*, the high altar, its reredos and setting, all date from this second period.

The choir of Cordova Cathedral (once the Great Mosque) was constructed by the Canons of the sixteenth century, but the stalls date from the eighteenth century, and are the work of Pedro Duque Cornejo, or were executed under his direction. Cornejo was born in Seville in 1677. He became the pupil and son-in-law of Pedro Roldán.

He worked for nine years on this *sillería*, and died in 1757, the year of its inauguration. The whole work comprises 63 high and 42 low stalls, as well as the thrones of the Bishop and of his acolytes. The carved scenes are taken from the Old and New Testaments and the lives of local saints.

The grandeur and importance of eighteenth-century Spain was for long little appreciated, owing both to the ignorance of foreigners and to the hostility of Spaniards towards a period when Frenchmen and Italians occupied the foreground of the scene at the Spanish Court. The decline of the country, its gradual sinking into mediocrity, seem undeniable, when compared with the political and military power of the reigns of Charles V and Philip II, and the intellectual and artistic flowering during the reign of Philip IV. The eighteenth century was long considered a period of almost shameful darkness, ending only with the dazzling genius of Goya.

Yet history reveals that Spain has no cause to blush for the eighteenth century. The Bourbon kings directed, or at least permitted, the political and economic reorganization of the kingdom. The greatest of them, Charles III (1716–1788), is one of the most engaging figures of enlightened despotism. While still young, this eldest son of Philip V and his second wife Elizabeth Farnese set off to claim in Italy the throne apparently barred to him in Spain. He reigned in Parma and, for twenty years, in Naples (1738–1759). Then, on the death of his brother Ferdinand, he at last succeeded to the throne of Spain. Surrounding himself with French and Italian artists, and enlisting in his personal service the Bohemian painter Mengs, he set about decorating the Royal Palace in Madrid, which had been begun by his father and continued by his brother.

145

146

149

150

151

159

160

161

162

Plates 9, 13, 16, 17, 21, 27, 30, 37, 39, 40, 41, 42, 43, 44, 49, 55, 67, 82, 89, 94, 95, 96, 97, 98, 99, 103, 104, 105, 106, 109, 110, 116, 117, 119, 122, 125, 126, 127, 132, 136, 137, 141, 142, 143, 144, 146, 148, 149, 151, 153, 156, 157, 158, 159, 161, 162, Photo Yan

Plates 2, 5, 6, 7, 14, 20, 22, 35, 36, 38, 47, 51, 52, 53, 56, 62, 65, 66, 68, 70, 71, 72, 74, 75, 77, 78, 79, 80, 81, 83, 85, 86, 87, 88, 90, 114, 115, 131, 135, 138, 139, 164, Photo André Martin

Plates 1, 15, 23, 25, 32, 54, 59, 61, 63, 76, 91, 92, 93, 100, 112, 113, 123, 124, Photo André Serres

Plates 24, 26, 28, 29, 31, 33, 34, 50, 57, 69, 147, 150, Photo Henri Bertault

Plates 4, 8, 10, 11, 12, 18, 19, 84, 108, Photo Antoine Trincano

Plates 3, 45, 46, 111, 128, 129, 130, 140, 145, Photo Mikaël Audrain

Plates 64, 73, 102, 107, 133, 134, Photo Yan-Zodiaque

Plates 118, 121, 154, 155, 163, Photo Molly

Plate 152, Photo Anderson; 160, Photo Arts Photomécaniques; 58, 101, Photo Colas; 120, Photo Librairie Tisné; 48, Photo Photo-Club Burgos; 60, Photo Rifaux

Index